ISBN 978-1-330-91556-1
PIBN 10120960

1 MONTH OF FREE READING

at

www.ForgottenBooks.com

By purchasing this book you are eligible for one month membership to ForgottenBooks.com, giving you unlimited access to our entire collection of over 700,000 titles via our web site and mobile apps.

To claim your free month visit:

www.forgottenbooks.com/free120960

Similar Books Are Available from
www.forgottenbooks.com

Ancient English

ȝ Week Ceremonial.

BY

HENRY JOHN FEASEY.

LONDON:

THOMAS BAKER, 1, SOHO SQUARE.

Contents.

The Ancient English Holy Week Ceremonial.

The Lenten Array.

THE spectacle presented to the eyes of the faithful in our *English* *Churches* in times anterior to the Reformation period in the Holy Season of Lent was one of exterior penitence. Not alone did the *Church* insist on the necessity of a sincere interior penitence, but also on the penance of the senses. Thus, in order that the minds of Her children should not be diverted from the sublime "PAGENTE OF THE PACION" of Her Divine Lord and Master, She shrouded Her altars, and covered up with veils Her sacred pictures and images; hushed the notes of Her organs, and stilled the music of Her bells.

In the first four weeks in Lent white linen or similar plain material was used by Her for the vesting of Her altars and Her priests, as typical of the purity and sincerity of repentance*; and from the Passion till the Vigil of Easter— the two last weeks in Lent—red cloth or a like stuff, pointing to the dust of Earth by the one, by the other the immortality of Heaven. While by a mystic combination of the two she continually reminded them, at this most solemn season of the whole Christian year, of the precious blood-shedding of the Pure and Immaculate Lamb of God.

With the same intention she also suspended the Lenten Veil between the Choir and the Altar—"the Veil," as the *Liber Festivalis* says, "that all this Lent hath been drawn between us and the choir betokeneth the Passion that was hid and unknown till the day came."

: Lenten ag.

Before proceeding to speak particularly of the Lenten Veil, the Rood Cloth, etc., it may be interesting to touch, somewhat lightly of necessity, on the several other parts of what was known as "the Lenten Array," which includes the vestments of the clergy, the ornaments or coverings for the altars, crosses, statuary, and pictures. The best and shortest way of doing this will be to give a few extracts from the old inventories and churchwardens'

---

* See *Lev.* xvi. 4.

accounts, merely premising that in the early days plain white linen was used as the material for vestments and coverings both of clergy and church ornaments*, which as time went on became more ornamental—the ground colour remaining generally white though the stuff was of silk, satin, velvet, and other rich material.

Thus we find in

> 1407. *Warwick College* (S. Mary's):
> "An hole vestiment of *white* tartaryn for lenton that is to say. iij aubes. iij amytes. wyth the parures. a chesible. iij stolis. iiij fanons. iij girdelis. ij auter clothis wyth a frontel. and a towail. iij curtyns. a lectron cloth. and a veyle of lynnen cloth."—*Chartulary of Warwick College*, f. ccij[b]. (Public Record Office.)

Here we not only find the "vestment" including the chasuble and all its appurtenances,—stoles, fanons (maniples), and girdles; but also altar cloths and curtains, frontal, towel, lectern-cloth and lent veil. We find also that

---

* Post completorium cruces pannis albis cooperiantur "et linteis."—*Ordinarius Cisterciensis*, printed by Dr. Rock. "Secunda feria prime ebdomade Quadragesime ad matutinas omnes cruces et imagines, et reliquie, . . . sint cooperta usque ad matutinas in die Pasche." **Registrum Osmundi**, § cii.

the amices appertaining to the albes, and doubtless the albes themselves, were apparelled, although the time of Lent :—

> 15th *century* King's College, Cambridge: "iiij aubes for childre. with parours according to the same for Lenton"—

and that in *practice*, whatever may have been ordered, the old *E*nglish colours for Lenten use were White and Red—*white* for the earlier part of that Season, with red crosses, and *red* for Passiontyde*. This has been abundantly proved by Mr. St. John Hope in his valuable paper on *The English Liturgical Colours* (S. Paul's *E*ccles. Society Trans., Vol. ii., p. 233), *e.g.* :—

> In 1453, the Lenten Array at *King's College, Cambridge,* included:
> " iij chesibles of bustian the orfrez of raied riban of threed iij aubes iij amities with parours stoles and phanons according to the same. viij aulter clothz of lynen cloth with reed crosez iij pair curteyns & j vail of the same j painted cloth to hange before the *C*rucifix ij baners of the same with figures of

---

* "*Red* albes for Passion Week " are specially mentioned at Peterborough. See *Gunton's* " *History of the Church of Peterborough.*"

the Passion for Lẹnton."—*Ecclesiologist,*
XX. 311-13.

At Ludlow (Whitefriars) Priory was "a
chasabull and ij decons of whyte nedell
work for Lent"; among the "Lent
stuff" in the "Vestry" of King Edward
VI. in 1547, "one Priest, Deacon, and
Sub-deacon of white Damaske with
redd Crosses"; and at St. Stephen's,
Coleman Street (1466), j hole sute of
vestments of whyte bustyan for Sundayes
in time of Lent with Rede Roses
embraudet."

Occasionally, among the numerous instances
of *white* vestures for clergy and altar, we come
across such as the following:

1453. *King's College, Cambridge.*

"iij dalmatiques of *reed* with aubes
amytes stoles and phanons and iiij aubes
for childre with parours according to
the same, for lenton."—*Ecclesiologist,*
XX. 311-13.

circa 1550. *Wingham College, Kent.*

"j vestyment of *redd* with a crosse of
blewe worsted used in Lente."—*Sacristy,*
i. 376.

temp. Edward VI., *York Minster.*

" A *blewe* vestement with two dalmaticks

for Lent."—*York Fabric Roles* (Surtees Soc.) xxxv. 312.

1552. *London. S. Paul's Cathedral Church.*

"*Item*, a vestment of *redde* silke for lente w^t two tunycles to the same."—*Ecclesiologist*, xvii. 203.

6. *Edward VI. Lewisham, Kent.*

"*Item*, one vestment of red velvet for the Lent."—Walcot. " *Church Goods in Kent.*"

This use of Red and Blue may possibly be explained by the following items :

1495. *Magdalen College, Oxford.*

"a *red* suit for *Sundays* in Lent time and "a dorsal and frontal of *blood-coloured* tewke (de sangwein tewke) for the high altar *Sundays* in Lent.—Hare *MS.*, 4240.

1506. *Exeter Cathedral Church.*

" blue clothes for the high altar, a large *purple* chasuble for *Sundays* in Lent and Advent."—*Oliver*, 328, &c.

The theory of red for Sundays in Lent finds also additional support from an event which occurred in East Anglia in the XV. century. In 1444 the city of Norwich, in defending itself against a charge of insurrection, protested that a certain gathering reported as a rising

was but a peaceful show wherein one Gladman
had only "made disport with his neighbours,
having his horse trapped with tynnsoyle and
other nice disguisy things, crowned as king of
Christmas, while before him went each Month
disguised after the season required, and Lent,
clad in *white, and red* herring skins and his horse
trapped with oyster shells, after him."*

Among the APPAREL FOR THE ALTAR we
find:

> 1368 + 1419. *Norwich. S. Lawrence.*
> "3 *white linen* cloths powdered with
> great red crosses of saye for the service
> of the same three altars with covers of
> the same suit for covering all the images
> in the church in the time of Lent."

> 1432. *Bristol. S. Nicholas.*
> "Item viij clothes of wyzht w^t crucyfyx
> for lent for iiij awters."—*MS. Inventory,
> S. Nicholas, Bristol.*

> 1440. *Somerby, Lincolnshire (ex dono* Sir
> Thomas Cumberworth).
> " All the array for Lenton for the altar
> both over dose and nether dose with
> curtines and fronturs all of lynnen

---

* Bloomfield, *Norfolk,* iii. 149-50, 154-5, quoted by Green, *Life in
the XV. Century.*

cloth."— Peacock. *English Church Furniture,* 182-3.

1470. *London. S. Margaret Pattens.*

"*Item* for the same (high) awter a ffronte & a nether fronte of *whyte* for lent.

"*Item* for the same awter (of our Lady) a ffronte & a nether ffronte *whyte* for lent w^t ij curteyns." — *Archæological Journal,* xlii. 317, 319.

In the great chapel of Cardl. Fisher was an altar hanging of white sarcenet with red say crosses.—*Inventory of goods confiscated* 27th April, 1534.

1539. *Peterborough Abbey.*

"*Item* one vestment of white fustian for Lent."

1544-5. *Oxford. S. Frideswide's Priory.* (Black Canons) Suppression.

"Hangings for the highe alter, for aboue and benethe, of new *whit* sercenett wth redd crosses, called alter clothes for Lentt. x^{d.}"—Dugdale, *Mon. Angl.* ii. 167.

1546. *London. S. Peter, Cornhill.* Among "the Apparell of the high awter."

"An awter clothe of *whyte* for Lent w^t crosses of red w^t ij curtens of *whyte*

lynnen."—Public Record Office. *Exch.*
Q. R. Misc. Ch. Gds. $\frac{4}{1.}$ $\frac{4}{47.}$

1550. (4 Ed. VI.) London. S. Dunstan
in the *E*ast.

The "Lent Vestments" and "Hangings"
were of white bustian and linen with red
crosses.—P.R.O. *Ch. Gds. Q. R.* $\frac{4}{98.}$

On the 27th March, A.D. 1536, the Commissioners engaged in taking an inventory of
the goods and chattels of the Benedictine
Nunnery of *Minster*, Isle of Sheppey, actually
found "upon the High Aulter iiij alter clothes
of lynyn one front for above and a nother for
byneth of lynyn with crosses red and blew for
the Lent."—Public Record Office. *Chapter
House Book.* A. $\frac{3}{12.}$

Although these Lenten adornments or rather
coverings were as a general rule of linen,
canvas, diaper, buckram, fustian, worsted, saye,
and such like, yet instances are not infrequently
met with where the material employed is specified as of silk, sendal, sarcenet, tartarin and
other rich stuffs, and the same applies likewise
to the ornamentation of this Lent Apparel which
though ordinarily plain are found in some
instances to have been decorated in a greater
or lesser degree. Plain crosses of red[1] or blue,
or both; spots of flames, drops of blood, the

[1] Each veil should have a red cross in centre. See many authorities quoted. Church of Our Fathers, vol. iv. p. 223.

Sacred Monogram and the instruments of the Passion seem to have been common ornaments. The following are a few from the inventories :

1432. *Bristol. S. Nicholas.*
"*Item* viij clothes of wyzht w^t *crucyfyx* for lent for iiij awters."—*MS. Inventory. S. Nicholas, Bristol.*

circa 1462. *Salisbury Cathedral.* (Lady Hungerford's Chantry.) Among the Foundress' gifts. " *Item,* Two Autar cloths for Lenten time, of Linnen Cloth ; *with crosses of Purple in every cloth, & a Crown of Thorns hanging upon the head of every Cross,* with a frontel to the same," &c.—Dugdale *Baronage,* iii. 208.

1466. *London. S. Stephen, Coleman Street.* "J hole sute of vestments of whyte bustyan for sondayes in tyme of lent w^t *Rede Roses* embraudet, with stoles &c. of the same sute."
" ij stayned (altar) clothes with the tokens of the Passion for tyme of Lent."
—*Archæologia,* l. 38.

1479-86. *London. S. Margaret Pattens.* " ij new awter clothes ffor Lenton on above the awter w^t *the crucifixe of our lord* and a nod^r beneyth the awter *with the sepulcur of our lord.*"—*Arch'l Journal,* xlii. 321.

1483. *London. S. Christopher le Stocks.* (Lente Clothes.)

" Item for the high Aulter ij clothes of whyte stayned *with the Sonne uppon them and a Crosse with scorges upon the other.*" —Freshfield. *Minutes of Vestry Meetings of S. Christopher le Stocks*, 68.

1503. *Reading. S. Lawrence,* (Berks).

" An aulter clothe stayned *w* an image of *o* lady of Pyte and ij angels* and a nother *w* the sepulchre and ij angells* for the hy awlter in lent."—Kerry, *Hist. of S. Lawrence, Reading.*

1509. *Will of Lady Margaret Beaufort.* Among other bequests to *Christ's College,* Cambridge.

" *Item* ij aulter clothes for lenten of white saten *with pagentes of the Pacion* in white and blake."—Cooper. *Memorial of Margaret, Countess of Richmond and Derby*, 131.

1529. *Long Melford, Suffolk.*

" One (altar cloth) for Lent *with whips and with angels.*"—Neale and Le Keux, *Churches in Great Britain*, vol. ii.

6. Edward VI. *Lewisham, Kent.*

" *Item* one sute of lenton clothes of white spotted with redd.

6. *Edward VI.* *London, S. Nicholas, Cole Abbey.*

"*E*ight altar cloths of white with drops of blood for Lent."—*Ecclesiologist*, xvii. 124-5.

It would appear that these Lent cloths for the altar and images were not infrequently made of *crysomes* returned to the church at the purification of women :—

1448. *Thame, Oxon.*

"A frontell w^t a clothe Bowyt y^t of Crysomys."

"*Item* a parell made of crysomes for lent."

"*Item* ij aut' clothes of crysomes for Lent time."*

---

* St. Gregory the Great calls the veil worn to preserve the chrism, birrus. It was white shot with red thread in memory of Christ's Passion.

The Lent Veil.

VEILS for the Chancel were coëval with the Earliest ages of the Christian religion. At first, doubtless in imitation of the Veil which shut off the Holy of Holies from the Holy Place both in the Jewish Tabernacle and Temple, they entirely shut off the chancel from the body of the Church, to be, as time passed on, reserved to the more immediate precincts of the altar itself which eventually came to be entirely surrounded with curtains or veils which were drawn aside only at certain portions of the Liturgy. The Lent Veil, though latterly restricted to the Lent season, was a survival of this ancient and more continuous custom of veiling the altar or sanctuary in earlier ages, a custom now practically obsolete in Western Christendom, though the iconostasis or solid Chancel Screen with its central doorway closed with curtains withdrawn at stated parts of the service, still in use among the Greeks, preserves essentially the same features.

The use in England of the Lent and other Veils in screening off the Sanctuary and covering up the sacred ornaments and imagery from Shrovetide to Easter goes back at least as far as the reign of Alfred, King of Wessex, who by his Code of *Ecclesiastical Laws* (Thorpe, *Ancient Laws and Institutes of England, London,* 1840, Vol. I.), published soon after his great victory over the Danes at the Battle of Ethundune (A.D. 878), decreed a fine of one hundred and twenty shillings for tearing down the holy veil in Lent, the obscuration of the altar during Lent being a custom greatly resented by the people.

The ancient rule of hanging the Lent Veil as well as of veiling pictures, images, and other church ornaments was from the first Monday after Ash Wednesday, *i.e.,* after Compline, or the first Evensong on the first Sunday in Lent until Easter in signification, *Durandus (Rat. Div. Off.* 1484)[1] says of the Veiling of the Godhead of Christ during the Passion.[2] The Church ornaments were thus veiled after Com pline from the fact that Lent did not always commence with Ash Wednesday. According to the *Ambrosian Rite* Ash Wednesday is not kept at all, their Lent beginning on the First Sunday in Lent—a sign of considerable

e also
e and
b's
duction.
one
d in
ce, he
it was
ractice to
a curtain
nt of the
, like the
en Veil.

antiquity—the distribution of ashes being put off until the Rogation Days which are observed on the Monday, Tuesday, and Wednesday in the week after Holy Thursday.

The Lent Veil, or *Velum Quadragesimale*,[3] was a large veil or curtain, or sometimes a pair, hung or stretched or drawn at that season of the year between the Quire and the Presbytery, and let down by a windlass, or hook, or drawn together by means of a line and pulley. In Cathedral churches it parted the Presbytery from the Quire. At *St. Paul's* it hung over the Quire step, whilst at *Salisbury* and *S. Alban's*, for instance, it depended between the Quire step and the Presbytery. In Parish Churches it separated the Chancel from the Nave. Beams of wood were in some cases placed across the front of the Sanctuary to support the Lent Veil, and traces of such may be seen at *Salisbury, Worcester,* and *St. Alban's* Cathedrals. In all probability the beam supporting the Great Rood was utilized in many instances for the purpose as in the *St. Alban's* example, where a portion of the old Rood Beam remains in this identical position. In other cases the Lent Veil was suspended by the aid of hooks, several of which rusted with age, still retain their original position in some of

[3] In Germany they were called 'fasting cloths.'

our ancient churches—*Durham* and *Winchester* Cathedrals for example. In the Cathedral of *Salisbury* and *Arundel* the pulleys used for tightening the rope from which the Veil was hung are still in evidence. Nichols in his *Illustrations* (p. 109) has "For a greate iron to hang the veil of the Chancel against Lent.

1459. *London. S. Michael, Cornhill.* (Churchwardens' Accounts.)
"ij^d for a lyne for the veyle atte the high aucter."—Waterlow. *S. Michael's, Cornhill.*

14. Henry VII. *Reading. S. Lawrence.* (Churchwardens' Accounts.)
"It payed for whip-cord to draw the cloth at the hy auter i$^{d.}$"

1521-2. *London. S. Andrew Hubbard, East Cheap.*
"paid for lyne for the Vale."

1527. *London. St. Mary Hill.*
For a great iron to hang the veil of the Chancel against Lent, j^s.

1535. *Thame, Oxon.*
"*Item* paid for a cord for the vayle ij^d.

1540. (27. Henry VIII.) *Ludlow.* (Churchwardens' Accounts.)
"*Item* payd for cordes to hange the clothe and to draue the clothe that

hangyth in the mydes of the heygh chancelle in the Lent. ij$^{d.}$

It would appear that the Veil was adjusted by means of weights, &c.

1559. *London. S. Christopher le Stock.*
"*Item*, ther is a Vaile Clothe to hange before the high aucter & therto longeth ij weights of leed iche of xxviij$^{li.}$

The Lent Veil was kept down the whole of Lent on ferias, and raised only at the reading of the *G*ospel at Mass, and let down again when the priest says the *Secreta* before the *Sursum Corda*, and so remained even at the *E*levation, to the end, except on festivals of the Double *C*lass and of Nine Lessons, when it was withdrawn for the whole day. On Wednesday in Holy Week, in the reading of the Passion, at the words "*And the veil of the Temple was rent in twain*" (S. Luke xxiii. 45), it was dropped and not put up again till the next year. Other mention is made of its being suffered to fall on *G*ood Friday at the words, "*they parted my raiment among them.*" (St. John xix. 24. *Ps.* xxii. 18.) At *Exeter* a deacon is said to have advanced towards it and tore it asunder with his hand or ripped it up with a knife.

The *Constitutions of Archbishop Gray* (1250) declare it to be the duty of the parishioners to provide a Lent Veil for their Churches.

The use of the Lent Veil survived the ravages of the Reformation, being hung at *Ludlow* in 1548, after the rood, images, &c., had been removed, and was utilized by the Reformers themselves, though not exclusively in the time of Lent. *Dr. John Edgeworth,* Canon of Salisbury, Wells, and Bristol; who lived in the reigns of Henry VIII., *E*dward VI., and Mary, dying in that of *E*lizabeth; referring to the many manners and divers ways of ministering the Communion in the various reigns mentions this usage of the Lenten Veil, thus:

> "And anon, that way [of driving people out of church, except ministers, that the Communion should not be commonly seen and worshipped] seemed not best, and therefore there was [sic] veils or curtains drawn, yea, and in some churches the very Lent Cloth or veil hanged up though it were with Alleluïa in the *E*aster time, to hide it, that no man should see what the priest did, nor hear what he said." (*Sermons,* ed. 1557.

Thus they, unintentionally no doubt, reverted to the most ancient Christian practice of veiling the altar at the celebration of the Eucharist. Another account (Wriothesley, II. p. 47.), referring to the alterations at the *Cathedral of St. Paul* at this time says:

> 11th June, 1550. At night the high altar in Paules Church was pulled down, and a Table set where the altar stoode, with a Vayle drawne beneath the Steepes," &c.

Numerous references to the Lent Veil are to be found in the old inventories of Church Goods and Churchwardens' Accounts of which the following will suffice:

> 1297. *Kensworth, Herts.*
> "Velum quadragesimale decens consutum cum bestiis de lineo panno."
> —MS. W. D. 16. ¡*penes. Dec. et Cap. S. Pauli*, f. 47[b.]

> *temp.* Henry VI. *Bridgewater. S. Kathe rine's aisle, Somerset.*
> "ij steyned clothes to stand bifor the Tablement in ye lent tyme."—*Proceed. Somerset, Arch. and Nat. Hist. Soc.,* vii. 102.

> 1431. *London. S. Peter, Cheap.*
> "j veile steynede w[t] j crosse of rede

for lent in the quere."—*Jour. Brit. Arch. Assoc.* xxiv. 158.

1448. *Thame, Oxon.*

"*Item* a white veyle for the Croce in lent tyme and ano*r* white veyle to be hangyng in the chauncell befor the hy aut*r* in lentyn tyme."—Lee. *Hist. and Antiq*s· *of Thame Church*, col. 35.

1454. *Bristol. S. Ewen* (destroyed). (Churchwardens' Accounts.)

"*Item* ye veyl, otherwise called ye lent Cloth, of white lynen cloth, with a cros of blue & ye lyne therto."—Nicholls and Taylor. *Bristol, Past and Present,* ii. 250.

1466. *London. S. Stephen, Colman Street.*

"*Item* j vayle for lent to be drawne be for the hy aut' of lynnen. with blac' crossis."

1485. *Leicester. Langley, S. Mary's* (Benedictine Nunnery).

"One white and two blew to clothings to kever and auter ye ymags in lenten seysyn, ij curten for ye quere."

1535. *Minster, Isle of Sheppey, Kent.* (Benedictine Nuns.)

"*Item,* one greate lent clothe of lynyn to draw overthwart the quyer in the lent."—Public Record Office. *Chapter House Book*, A $\frac{3}{12}$.

1537. *Stanlaw Abbey, Cheshire.* (Cistercian.) "On olde hangyng for lent to hange before the alter."—P. Record Office. *Exch. Q.A. Mis. Ch. Gds.* $\frac{10}{29}$.

1545. *Poole. S. James, Dorset.* "*Item* a uayle to be hongyd vppon yᵉ lent afor yᵉ hye awter."—Sydenham, Hist. of Poole. 313.

3. *Edward* VI. *London. S. Dunstan in the East.*
"A greate Vale that was drawn before the highe Aulter, in Lente, wᵗ dyverse other thinges as Towelles, Aulter Cortyns, and Curtyns drawne before the paynture at the Aulter ends &ᶜ·"
—P. R. Office. *Ch. Gds. E*xch. R. R. $\frac{4}{98}$.

1550. *London. S. Michael, Cornhill.* (Churchwardens' Accounts.)
"XVˢ received for a Lenton cloth."

The inventories taken in 1552 (6. *E*dward VI.) give abundant examples of the Lent Veil:
Brightwalter, Berks.
'a old vayle of lynen clothe to hange overthwart Chaunsell.'
Yattendon, Berks.
'a clothe called A vayle colthe of

lynnene & lyned w^t blewe lynene wch was wonte to be drawene before the heyghe Alter in the lente time.'*

Hothfield, Kent.

'*Item* a lynnen cloth called a waylle.'

Lewisham, Kent.

'*Item* on vale cloth pictured with the Passion of lynnen with red spots.'

Bermondsey, Surrey.

'*Item* a olde vaylle y^t went over the quyer for Lent.'

Carshalton, Surrey.

'*Item* a lenton clothe to hang before the highe aulter.'†

Farnham, Surrey.

'A clothe of lynnen called a vale clothe.'

Farley, Surrey.

'*Item* a lente clothe of canvass steyneed with blue and red spottes.'†

Frensham, Surrey.

'j white Lent clothe.'†

Mitcham, Surrey.

'A drawing Lent clothe' sold.

Puttenham, Surrey.

'*Item* a white vayle clothe.'

---

* Money, Church Goods in Berks.
† ? Altar clothes or frontals.

Wandsworth, Surrey.

'*Item* a curtaine to draw in the chauncell.'

Wimbledon, Surrey.

'*Item* a Lenton clothe to drawe befor the altar.'‡

1557. (Last year of Q. Mary.) *London. S. Michael, Cornhill.*

" Paid for a Veile before the Hight Altar this Lente xxij^{s.} iiij^{d.}—*Church-wardens' Accounts.*

1560. *Chelmsford, Essex.*

" A vayle clothe for Lent."—*Tr. Essex Arch. Soc.*, ii. 216.

1565. (7. *Elizabeth.*) *Little Bitham, Lincolnshire.*

"*Item* . . . one veale in the chauncell."
—Peacock. *English Church Furniture.*

Although as a general rule the Lent Veil as well as the other Lenten coverings or ornaments were of plain unadorned stuffs such as fustian, canvas, linen, and the like, yet they were not always of mean and common material, but on the contrary, sometimes of silk, bandekin, samite, tartarin and other rich fabrics, thus :

---

‡ Daniel Tyssen, *Church Goods in Surrey.*

1222. *Salisbury Cathedral.*

" one Lenten Veil of silk." *(Velum unum de serico Quadragesimale.) Reg. S. Osmundi.*—Rolls Series, ii. 131.

Ante 1462. *All Souls' College, Oxford.*

" *Item* 1 Velum de serico et 1 de panno lineo 1 descloth cum rubea cruce pro XL."—Gutch. *Collect. Curiosa,* ii. 263, et seq :

1533. *Lindisfarne Priory, Holy Island.* (*A Cell to Durham.*)

" One veil for the quire in Lent of blacke silke."—Raine. *North Durham,* 125.

circa 1540. *Westminster Abbey* (Lent Stuffs.)

"A white clothe of sylk with a red cross servyng for Lent."—*Tr. Lond. and Midx. Arch. Soc.,* iv. 327-8.

Among the Ornaments of "The Vestry" of King *E*dward VI., late Henry VIII.'s Lenton Stuff: "Item one vaill of white sarcennet with a redd crosse of Sarcennet."—*Soc. Antiq., Lond. MS., cxxix. ff.* 466[b], 467.

Neither were these Lent Veils and other coverings without adornment with needlework, embroidery, and painting or staining, nor were they of any special colour, but of various, for

although white was prevalent, instances are on
record of their being of *White* and *Blue*, "paled
or striped,"—a somewhat usual combination—
Red and *White*, *Black* or *Black* and *Tawny;*
Green or *Green* and *Red;* and *Green* and *Yellow*,
or of *Yellow* and *Blue* Silk as at *Westminster* in
1388. In the year 1540 it is there stated to
have been of *Purple* In 1533, as we have
seen, at *Lindisfarne Priory*, it was of *Black*
silk.

> 1297. *Thorpe-le-Soken, Essex.* (White
> and Blue.)
> "Velum quadragesimale de panno lineo
> stragulato albo et blueto cum rosis."—
> *MS. W. D.* 16. *penes Dec. et Cap. S.
> Pauli*, f. 47[b.]
> 1384-5. *Windsor. S. George's Chapel.*
> (Blue and White.)
> "*Item* unum velum quadragesimale
> palleum, blodium, et albi coloris cum
> gartiers et aquilis auro pondratus."—
> Dugdale. *Mon. Angli.*, vi. 1363, 1366.
> 1388. *Westminster Abbey.* (Yellow and
> Blue.)
> "De velo et pannis quadragesimalibus.
> "Velum est unum *pro magno altari* de
> serico in media divisum Croced et blodii
> coloris," etc.—*MS. Inventory, penes Dec.
> et Cap. Cantuar.*

At St. Faith's, near St. Paul's, in 1295 was a Lent Veil of *Yellow* and Purple cloth, and at *E*xeter "a fair noble and precious Lenten Veil."

1454. *Will of William Halifax of Nottingham.* (White and Blue.)

"Lego j steyned cloth of white and blew that is writyn on Soli deo Honor *et* gloria to Seynt Mary auter (in St. Mary's Church, Nottingham) to hynge in tyme of Lenton before ye auter."
—*Test. Ebor.* (Sur. Soc. 30.) 172.*

1467-8. *Launceston, Cornwall.* (In the Accounts.) (Blue.)

"Blewe bokerham for the layent clothe."
—Peter's *Hist. of Launceston,* 149.

1470. *London. S. Margaret Pattens.* (White and Blue.)

"*Item* a Cloth of whyte and blew called a vayle for lent."—*Archl. Jl.,* xlii. 317-19.

circa 1540. *Westminster Abbey.* (Lent Stuff.) (Green—Purple.)

" A Travers of grene sylk.*

---

* It is difficult to distinguish in some instances whether an Altar Frontal or a Lent Veil or other hanging is intended in consequence of the loose and scrappy way in which the items are set down. Thus the 1534 Inventory of the Guild of the *Blessed Virgin Mary at Boston, Lincolnshire*, has, "*Item* iij quartars of a yard of blak sarcnett hangynge before the altar," which in modern measurement would answer neither purpose.

"ij drawyng perpull curteyns for the vayle before the highe awter."—*Tr. Lon. and Mid'x Arch. Soc.*, iv. 327-8

circa 1540. *Westminster. S. Stephen's Chapel.* (Red and White.)

"*Item* a vayle of red and whit s^{r}cenet for lent."—*Tr. Lon. and Mid'x Arch. Soc.*, iv. 369-70.

1543. *York Minster. S. Wilfrid's Chantry.* (Black and Tawny.)

"A Lent cloth of blacke and tawne sarsenet."—York Fab. Rolls. (Sur. Soc. 35.) 305.

1548. *London. S. Olave, Upwell.* (Old Jewry.) (Green and Red.)

"A curtayene of grene and red saye to draw ov' whart the quere."—Public Record Office. *Exch. Q.R. Mis. Ch. Goods*, $\frac{4}{1}$. $\frac{4}{47}$.

1550. (4 Ed. 6.) *London. S. Dunstan in the East.* (Green and Yellow.)

"*Item* a Vale of grene and yelowe Lynnen to drawe afore the highe Aulter." —P. Record Office. *Ch. Gds. Exch. Q.R.* $\frac{4}{98}$.

1552. (6 Ed. vi.) *Erith, Kent.* (White and Blue.)

"A vaile of lynnen cloth for lente of white and blewe."—*Arch. Cant.* viii. 150.

1552. *Boxford, Berks.* (White and Blue
paned.)
" A lent vayle before the highe aulter
w^t paynes blewe and white."—Money.
Church Goods in Berks, 6.

1552. *Farley, Surrey.* (Blue and Red
spotted.)
" A Lent clothe of canvas Steyned
with blew and red spottes."—Tyssen-
Amherst. *Church Goods in Surrey*, 57.

1552. *Bromley, Kent.* Lent Veil of linen
cloth. Walcott. *Church Goods in Kent.*
" A vale cloth pictured with the Passion
of lynnen with red spots."—Walcott.
Parish Church Goods in Kent.

At times the Veil was still more ornate, *e.g.:*

1529. *Long Melford, Suffolk.*
" A Clothe of Adam and Eve, to draw
before the High Altar in time of Lent
called the Veil."—Neale and Le Keux.
Churches in Great Britain, vol. ii.

Baleth (Durand, Rat. Div. Off., 1562) says in
Lent two veils were used, one round the choir
and the other before the altar, which were folded
back on Sundays, and at Tenebræ on Maundy
Thursday all were removed, in memory of the
rending of the Temple veil, except one altar

cloth, which commemorated the seamless vestment of *C*hrist.

The "Pepla" not only included the Lent Veil but likewise the *C*lothes or Veils used in covering or muffling up the crosses, images, and other ornaments of the *C*hurch, *i.e.*—the great *C*ross in the Rood Loft and the other crosses in the *C*hurch, the Pyx or vessel containing the *Æ*ucharist, the relics, the pictures, and imagery—all of which were veiled on the Monday of the First Week in Lent, and continued so covered up until Mattins early on *Æ*aster morning. (*Tract. S. Osmundi*, cap. 102, *apud Rock.*, iv. *p.* 68), except upon Palm Sunday when all *C*rosses were uncovered and exposed from the Fourth Station in the procession until after *Æ*vensong.

The Fifth Sunday in Lent was called *Dimanche Reprus*, from the veiling of the images; in *G*ermany, *Black* Sunday, from the veiling of the crosses, when the words of the *G*ospel are read, "Jesus hid Himself."

Altars, crosses, images, *etc.*, were veiled because the Scripture was concealed in the Prophets till the coming of *C*hrist,* and their

---

* A black veil for the head is used by the *Greek* priests in reading the Prophecies, in allusion to 2 Cor. iii. 13-16. See note "*peplum.*"

removal the manifestation by the Temple Veil being rent in twain. Of this covering of crosses and images, *Cranmer* (*circa* 1541) says:

"with the uncovering of the same at the resurrection, signifies not only the darkness of infidelity which covered the face of the Jews in the Old Testament, but also the dark knowledge that they had of Christ, who was the perfection and end of the law, and not yet opened until the time of His death and resurrection. The same is partly signified by the veil which hid the secret of the Holy of Holies from the people."[1]

Becon says that they were covered to stir the people to repentance, that they might "be found worthy against *Easter, i.e.* against the time of passing and going out of this world, clearly to behold and openly to see in the kingdom of heaven the shining face of God and His Saints; to declare the mourning and lamentation of sinners for their ungodly manners, the clothes that are hanged up in church have painted on them nothing else but the pains, torments, passion, blood-shedding, and death of Christ, that the mind should be fixed only on the Passion of Christ."[2]

nmer.
ts.

er Soc.,
  See also
er, vol. V.
6-24.

rly
ings,
er Soc.,

Beleth also mentions a veil which was removed from the front of the crucifix, behind which a pall was set, to show that the mystery of the passion had been made manifest. In some Churches banners of triumph were hung about the cross.

The Rood Cloth and Clothes for Images and Pictures.

THE principal cloth among the "Pepla" after the Lent Veil was

The Rood *or Rode Cloth, i.e.,* a veil or hanging drawn in front of the rood loft, so as to cover the *Great Rood* or crucifix standing in it. Other names for this cloth were the *Cross Cloth* and "*Shriving*" *Cloth*, for it would seem from *Raineri*, a monk of Liege, that the Lent Veil sometimes answered the double purpose both for *Chancel* and *Rood Cloth*. In the description he gives of the fall of a thunderbolt on the Church of his monastery, in 1182, he says :

"The lightning, entered by the door and leaping over the Lenten curtains which hung over the *Great Crucifix* and before the *Chancel* it darted to and fro," *etc*. It probably gained its name "*Shryving Cloth*" from the old custom of confessing and shriving church-folk in this place.

The "*Revelation to the Monk of Evesham,*" 1482—(Arber, *English Reprints*), would also lead to the conclusion that in some instances the Great Rood itself was taken down during Lent, and put away, in the *E*vesham instance, behind the altar.

Like the wide curtains at the *C*hancel arch the Rood *C*loth and clothes for covering the images, etc. were either of linen or silk, and though usually white—sometimes called "ashen" from the linen being unbleached,— was not always so. The usual colour for the Rood *C*loth appears to have been either white, green, or red, especially in Herts, Kent, and other southern counties, and the clothes for images frequently blue, or black and white, all the white clothes being embroidered in the centre with red equally limbed crosses, and when darker colours were used the crosses were frequently white. It would also appear that at times other than linen, *etc.* was used, as for example:

> 1249. *Willesden, Parish Church.*
>
> "A Lenten Veil, old and worn, and *a veil* of *netted wool* for covering the *C*ross in the *C*hurch."

The Rood *C*loth, as the Lenten Veil, was suspended by a line across the *C*hurch, and

lowered or drawn up or aside with pulleys. A
curtain of this kind is frequently mentioned
in the *Leverton, Lincolnshire,* and other Church
Accounts :

> 1524. *S. Lawrence, Reading.*
>
> " For a lyne to pull upp the clothe before
> the rode, ij$^{s.}$ vi$^{d.}$"
>
> 14 Henry VII. " *Item* payd for lyne to
> draw the curtens in the same [rode] loft,
> iij$^{d.}$"—*S. Lawrence, Reading,* Church-
> wardens' Accounts.
>
> 1545 (36 Henry VIII). *Ludlow.*
>
> " *Item,* for settynge up of a loker to
> drawe the corde before the crucifixe, j$^{d.}$"
> —*Churchwardens' Accounts.*

The Rood Cloth was frequently called the
CROSS CLOTH, and from the exceptionally large
number of them found enumerated in the old
Inventories and Church Accounts the term
must have been applied to clothes other than
that hanging before the Great Rood. Many
of the clothes so called were probably those
which covered the images and pictures deriving
their appellation from the crosses embroidered
on them. Again, in the inventories such items
as the following often appear :

> 6. Edward VI. *Lewisham, Kent.*
>
> " *Item,* one crosse of latten with ij

clothes of grene silke."—Walcot. *Church Goods in Kent.*

3rd Elizabeth. *Astrape, Lincolnshire.*
" *Item,* a crosse and a crosse clothe."

1565. *Basingham, Linc.*
" *Item,* one crosse w^t a crosse cloth."

1565. *Belton in the Isle of Axholme, Linc.*
" *Item,* one crosse of wood and one crosse cloth."

1566. *Braughton, Linc.*
" *Item,* a crose clothe and a cross."

1565. *Castlebyth, Linc.*
" *Item,* for o^r crosse and crose clothes."
—Peacock. *Eng. Ch. Fur.*

In fact the cross,—evidently the processional cross, (and the altar cross was frequently used, by being attached to a staff, for processions), and not the *Great Rood*,—is generally accompanied by its *cloth,* used most likely as a sudary or vexillum as with the pastoral staves of bishops, or perhaps again even as banners, and there is such a mention of one so hung to a cross. The 1566 Inventory of *Welbie, Lincolnshire,* has both Rood Cloth and Cross Cloth and other linen " bagdig" sold, &c. Thus many would be accounted for.

The inventories 'give the following examples of the Rood or Cross and other clothes :

1222. *Sarum Cathedral.*

lum, a ilso d to the ʒorn over ul iress of if III.

"One peplum[1] of red silk [Lent Veil]; five pepla of white silk; three of linen for the images; two curtains to cover over the crosses in Lent; two more for the cross over the principal altar; one for the cross near the South door."

1354 (?). *Hulne Priory, Northumberland.* (White Friars.)

"Sex panni albi cruce rubea signati, canobio novo duplati, pro tribus altaribus in Quadragesima, septimus pro pulpito, octavus pro cruce, nonus pro nᵒ ejusdem, decimus pro velo ejusdem sectæ."— *Harl. MS.*, 3897.

1388. *Westminster Abbey.*

"De velo et pannis quadragesimalibus "Velum est unum pro magno altari de Serico in medio divisum Crocei et blodii coloris et vj alii panni quadragesimales quo primus pannus lineus latus cum signis Dominicæ passionis pro cruce velanda. Secundus et tertius pro ymaginibus apostolorum Petri et Pauli velandis. Quartus et quintus pro costis magni alteris. Sextus longus pro trabe sub pede Crucifixi velanda."—*MS. In-ventory, penes Dec. et Cap. Cantuar.*

1431., *London. , S. Peter, Cheap.*

"*Item,* j clothe of blacke longynge to the beme w^t dyv'rs armes of lords."[2]

1470. (10 Ed. IV.) *London, S. Margaret Pattens.*

"*Item,* a new crosse clothe of ye assupcon of o^r lady w^t saynt margett & saynt Kat'yn and w^t ye v woundes of o^r lord the ground y' of is gren sarsenett and ij smale belles on ye staffe." [This "Cross Cloth" was evidently a banner as perhaps the others.] Another "Cross Cloth" was "steyned with the Resurrecion," a "Roode Clothe" "steyned with S. Margaret," another with the Passion of our Lord. There was also one "Roode Cloth" afore the rood in Lent, or again as at *Horton Kirby, Kent,* (6 Edward VI.): "*Item,* a crosse cloth of grene sarcenet of th' Assumpcon of our Ladye with aungells of gold." "*Item,* on other crosse cloth of white tuke with an aungell on it."

1473. *S. Mary's, Sandwich.*

"*Item,* ij towells for the crossis."

1479. *Cobham College, Kent.*

"*Item,* velum lineum pro Quadragesima cum panno pro Crucifixo."

[2] Accounts of Lee, Kent, (6. Ed. 6.), have "*Item.* a painted clothe upon the rode lofte with Jesus in the mydest." The "rude cloth" at *S. Mary, Addington, Surrey,* had the "xij apostalles payntyd."

"*Item,* ij panni de albo serico cum bina cruce de rubeo pro Quadragesima."
—Thorpe, *Registrum Roffense,* 240. 1.

1485. *Canterbury. S⸱ Andrew. Kent.*
"*Item,* j lynnyn cloth to hang afore the cross in the forechirche tempore, xlme."
—*Arch. Cant.* xvii. 151.

1506. *Exeter Cathedral Church.*
" Panni quadragesimales :
" 1 pannis lineus stayned cum cruce et aliis signis de Passione Domini pro cruce cooperienda in choro.
" 1 pannus stragulatus cum magna rubea cruce per medium operatus cum leopardis glauci coloris pro magna cruce cooperienda."—Oliver. 362.

1538. Salisbury. (Black Friars.)
" A gret meny of clotheis for lent."
" A grit clothe to hange before ye rode."
—*Wilts. Arch. & Nat. Hist. Mag.* xii. 361.

circa 1540. *Westminster Abbey.* (Lent Stuff.)
" A gret clothe paynted for the crucifix over the highe awter."
" A staynyd clothe ffor the Crokyd Rood."
—*Trans. Lon. & Midx. Arch. Soc.,* iv. 327-8.

1549. (3. Ed. VI.) *London. S. Dunstan in the East.*

" A greate cloth that dyd hange before the Roode in the Lente."—Public Record Office. *Ch. Gds. Exch.* Q. R. $\frac{4}{98}$.

1552. (6. Ed. VI.) An inventory of Church Goods in the ounty of *Herts*, mentions:

" iiij sheets that did hange befor the tabernacles*; a Canopie of linnen, and 10 peces of linnen that covered the tabernacles; ij clothes that hanged befor pillors; a cloth of the Passion; an *old* coverlet [pro ecclesia]†; a coveringe lynede with lynen, and another unlyned; one sheet of Holland cloth, etc."

1552. (6. Edward VI.) *All Saints, Canterbury, Kent.*

" Twenty five peces of lenton clothes." —Walcot. *Church Goods in Kent.*

1552. Boxford, Berks.

" A lynyne clothe to drawe before the Roode."—Money. *Ch. Gds. in Berks.*

---

* Curiously enough a MS. Inventory of *Lechworth, Worcestershire,* has a similar entry : " iiij shettis aft dyd hange before ye tabernacles."

† Ornaments of all kinds, including vestments " old," " worn," and " in dekay" were always left " for the Church " by Edward VI.'s Commissioners, thereby having the real motive for the spoliation.

1559. (1. *Eliz.*) *London. S. Christopher le Stock.*

"A cloth to hange before the Rood with the Passion Story."

1565. (7: *Eliz.*) *Hollywell, Lincolnshire.*

"*Item*, one vale that honge before the rood broken and defaced."—Peacock. *Eng. Ch. Furniture.*

As has been shown these Rood and other clothes were not confined to one colour nor on the other hand devoid of adornment. Many of them were painted:

1547. *Thame, Oxon.*

"Paid to painter for painting Vayle before the Rood. viij^d."

1555. *Ludlow.* (Churchwardens' Accounts.)

"For painting the cross cloth vj^s viij^d" And similar entries are frequent in the inventories, etc.; *e.g.*: "A painted cloth," "16 peces of painted clothes," "viij Curtens of lynnyn cloth painted for lent," "one sute of lenten clothes of white spotted with redd," "one small pece of white Sarcennet wth a redd Crosse painted with five woundes," "vij lynen altar clothes* with redd roses, for Lent,"

---

* The term "altar cloth" has a wide application and would often include many things beside the mere frontal, *e.g.*: 1368—1419. *Norwich. S. Lawrence.* "3 white linen clothes powdered with great red crosses of saye for the service of the same three altars with covers of the same suit for covering all the images in the Church in the time of Lent." —*Test. Ebor. iii.* (Sur. Soc. 45.) 13.

"Certeyn linnen clothes for the Lent," "iiij payntid clothis for Lent," "xxxiij newer lenteyn clothes; j w^t curteyns for the aulters and imagies of dyvers pyctories of the passion of Cryste." The Rood Cloth of S. Stephen, Coleman Street (1466), was stained with the Passion of our Lord; that at S. Christopher le Stock had a green fringe.

> 1440. Will of Sir Thomas Cumberworth. Bequest to *Somerby Church, Lincolnshire.* "*Item*, a stened Cloth wth byrdes of golde for the rood loft."—Peacock. *Eng. Ch. Furniture.*

> 1534. *Boston, Lincolnshire.* "*Item*, a crosse cloth of white sarcynett w^t an ymage of our ladye w^t divers angelles and pictures."—Inventory of Goods of *Guild of the B.V. Mary of Boston.*
> "*Item*, an olde crosse cloth of sarcynett w^t the ymage of our lady thereon stayned."—*Ibid.*

> 1552 (6. Ed. VI.). *Beatherisden, Kent.* Cross cloths were of sarcenet with our Lady and angels thereon; at *All Saints', Canterbury*, of silk, with the Trinity and Assumption.

1552. *London. S. Nicholas. Cole Abbey.*
"A Cross cloth of green silk with a picture of Jesus and the Fishmongers' Arms."

"A Cross cloth of white sarsnet with a picture of our Lady and Gabriel."

1566. *Gretford, Lincolnshire.*
"*Item*, a crosse clothe of grene silke w^t the Image of the trynytie yet re-mayninge."—Peacock. *Eng. Ch. Fur.*

As to colour the following will suffice:

1552. *Broxbourne, Herts.*
"*Item*, one Crosse Clothe of donne Sarsnett fryned, with a pykture on both sydes alyke."

1552. *Ashford, Kent.*
"One crosse clothe of grene sylke."

Ash, Kent.
"One crosse clothe of red silk."

Beckenham, Kent.
"ij clothes for the crosse thone of grene sarcenett thother of paynted cloth."

Bethersden, Kent.
"A crosse clothe of sarcenat with ye pyctor of our Ladye and aungells thereon."

Bexley, Kent.

" ij clothes for the Crosse, one of red sarcenett, thother of grene silke."

Brabourne, Kent.

"a crosse cloth of red silk & another of Russett."

Bylsington, Kent.

" a crosse cloth of grene silke."

Chislehurst, Kent.

" j pece of red velvett for the crosse on Good Fridaye."*

Cheam, Surrey.

' a cloth steyned to hang upon the rood.'

1566.   *Welbie, Lincolnshire.*

" *Item*, a crosse clothe of grene sesynet defaced."

It will be noted that the material employed was frequently either silk or sarcenet, indeed of fifty found enumerated in the 1552 Inventory taken for the County of Herts., nearly *all*, where the material is named, were of *silk*, the few exceptions being of *sarcenet*. It may not be at all improbable that some of the more elaborately embroidered or painted of these Cross Cloths were banners as the example at

---

* The Accounts of S. Margaret's, Westminster, have a like item under the 2nd year of Edward VI., " *Item*, a rede Ondarye for the Crosse," probably an under cloth.

S. Margaret Pattens, or Clothes for the further decoration of the Rood and Rood Loft on Festivals, as the "steyned cloth wth byrdes of Golde for the rood loft," at *Somerby Church, Lincolnshire,* and not for veiling the rood in Lent.

The following are a few of the items especially relating to the coverings for images and pictures:

> 1350. (24 Ed. III.) Inventory of Articles in *Chapel of London Bridge.*
> " One veil for Lent, two linen cloths for covering the cross, and the image of St. Thomas before the altar."

> 1429. *S. Alban's Abbey, Herts.* (Altar of S. Lawrence.)
> " *Item* duo panniculi albi cum Quinque Plagis Christi desuper staynati pro coopertura ymaginum Sanctorum Laurentii et Grimbaldi tempore Quadragesimali." — Anumdesham's *Annales Mon. S. Albani,* Rolls Series, i. 450.

> *temp.* Henry VI. *Bridgewater* (S. Katherine's aisle), *Somerset.*
> " A clothe to sett before Seynt Katryn in the lent time."—*Proc. Somerset Arch. and Nat. Hist. Soc.,* vii. 102.

1447. *Thame, Oxon.*

"A clothe of blewe card to·cu're the ymages in lent w^t ij custos of the same." —Lee. *Hist. and Antiq. of Thame Church,* col. 35.

1450. *S. Ewen, Bristol.*

"One clothe to couer the rood yn lent tyme aboue, one cloth to couer rood in Seynt Johns is Chapel, one cloth to couer our Ladye, Seynt Anne, Seynt John yn the seid chapel with the baner of Seynt George to couer the Trinite ouer the rood in the same chapel."

circa 1462. *Salisbury Cathedral Church.* (Lady Hungerford's Chantry.) Among the Foundress's gifts :

"*Item,* Two Curtains of Linnen Cloth, to cover the Images with in the Lent, of elle broad Cloth ; two leves of bredth, and three yardes of length."

"*Item,* An Hanging of Linnen Cloth, to cover the pictures of the chappel in Lent time, round about from the one arch to the other."—Dugdale. *Baronage,* iii. 208.

1485. *Langley Priory, Leicestershire.* (Benedictine Nuns.)

"J white and ij blew clothys to kever

and auter ye ymages in lenten seysyn."

"ij curten for ye quere."

"xviij pesys of lynyne to kever ye ymages with in ye same sesyne."—*Assoc^d. Socs. Rpts.*, xi. 203.

Fifteenth Century English Psalter. Inventory on a flyleaf.

"*Item*, ij curtens of whit steyned for the images in taber[nacles]."—*Notes and Queries*, MS. ix. May 3rd, 1890.

circa 1500. *York Minster.*

"Pro summo altari Duæ peciæ de albo panno lineo cum cruce rubea pro quadragesima et duabus curtinis.

"Panni pendentis pro choro, Unus pannus del bokerham coloris blodii pro coopertura Sancti Petri in quadragesima." [Unus pannus de bokeram, coloris blodii, pro coopertura ymaginis B.M.]—*York Fab. Rolls.* (Sur. Soc. 35.) 227.

1521. *Reading. S. Lawrence.*

"*Item*, paid for canvas for cov'ing of Seynt Michell, iij^d." — *Churchwardens' Accounts.*

1. *Edward VI. Rainham, Essex.*

"A napkyn of sylke, a Roode Clothe, or olde clothes y^t covered ye ymages in Lent & y^e vayle."—*Sold by Churchwardens.*

1539. *Peterborough Abbey.* (Infirmary Chapel.)

" *Item,* old clothes to cover Saints in Lent."

1549. (3. Ed. VI.) *London. S. Dunstan in the East.*

"Curtyns drawne before the paynture at the Aulter ends," &c.—Public Record Office. *Ch. Gds.* *E*xch. R. R. $\frac{4}{98.}$

1552. (6. Ed. VI.) *Lewisham, Kent.*

" Three clothes to hange on Santes of lynnen cloth."

These clothes as has been said were generally plain or marked with red crosses, but in some instances they were more ornate, *e.g. :*

1431. *London   S. Peter, Cheap.*

Besides the " ij clothes w^t rede crosses for Peter and Paule to kyuer heme in lente," there were clothes of the same (Lent) suite " with a hede," " with lilies," " with M crowned for our lady," " with j sword and j whele," " with a castle for S. Barbara," " with j pair of bedes for S. Sythe," " with a hed for S. Dunstan," and " with a mitre for S. Nicholas." Ten painted Lenten clothes were at St. Mary's, Newington, Surrey.—Tyssen. *Church Goods of Surrey.*

1466. *London. S. Stephen, Coleman Street.*

"*Item,* one covering for the Christ stayned with the Trinity in the midst and full of angels."

1559. *London. S. Christopher le Stock.*

"*Item,* ij clothes with. the Image of Seynt Cristofre to couer Seynt Cristofre."

1479-86. *London. S. Margaret Pattens.*

"*Item,* a covyr ffor ye sakyrment or ffor the best crosse off changeabull sylke."

1511. (3. Hy. VIII.) *London. St. Margaret Pattens.*

"*Item,* a clothe for lent to hange before the Srivyng pewe."

At Winchester College a canopy of linsey-woolsey, powdered with stars of gold used to fall over the pyx on Palm Sunday and Corpus Christi.

That these clothes were of some value as well as ornament is proved by the fact that the churchwarden at *Tallington, Lincolnshire,* took the Cross Cloth and·hung it in his hall, while that of *Stallingbrook,* in the same county was sold to some strolling players.

The author of the *Beehive of the Romish Churche,* (1580. fo. 190^b·) says:

"The whole of Lent through they doe cause their images to looke through a blewe cloth," thus inferring the linen used was generally of a blue colour.

A Rational or explanation of ceremonies drawn up probably in 1541, (given in *Collier*, vol. v. pp. 106-24), states among other things that " the covering of the cross and images in Lent, with the uncovering of the same at the Resurrection is a very good usuage."

N.B.—The reredos if not closed with shutters would be covered with a veil of unbleached linen, and perhaps embroidered with the instruments of the Passion.

All crosses are unveiled for the Palm Sunday procession, and remain so until after *E*vensong.

The Lent Cross.

A SPECIAL Cross, to head the processions, was reserved for Lent. It was of wood, and generally as at Sarum, painted blood-red and without the figure of the Crucified Redeemer. "Deferatur crux lingea rubri coloris depicta sine ymagine crucifixi."—*Crade michi*, quoted by Rock in "Church of our Fathers," Vol. iv. p. 226. Sir Thomas More, we are told by *Cresacre More* his great grandson, walked to the block "carrying in his hand a red cross."* *Piers Plowman* too in his 'Vision' speaks of him who came in with a cross painted all bloody. Christ's arms, his coat armour. "Christ with his cross, conqueror of Christine." On the other hands the inventories tell us the Lent crosses at St. Margaret Pattens and St. Peter Cheap were *green*† in colour :

* Rock, *Church of our Fathers*, Vol. iv., p. 226.

† A *green* cross was borne before the Grand Inquisitor of the Holy Office and the Flagellants bore red crosses aloft. A black sword is used by the Lord Mayor in Lent, public fast days, and on the death of any of the Royal Family.

1486. *London. St. Margaret Pattens.*
"A crosse and a crossè staffe to serve for lentten, paynted green withoute ymages w^t iij white silver nailes."
—*Arch. Journal* xlii., p. 322.

1531. *London. St. Peter Cheap.*
"*Item*, paid for payntynge 'the grene crosse' for Lent ij^d."

1466. *London. St. Stephen, Coleman Street.*
"*Item*, ij crosses of tre o^n of them for to be borne in pcess^{on} in tyme of lent."

1555. *London. St. Michael, Cornhill.*
(Churchwardens' Account.)
"Paide for a Crosse and a staffe for Lente of wood xij^d."

1555. *London St. Peter Cheap.*
"*Item*, payd for makynge and payntynge of a lenten crosse."

Special banners would appear also to have been reserved for this season

1527. *London. St. Andrew Hubbard, East Cheap.* (Churchwardens' Account.)
"Payd ffor iiij knopes ffor the passion baneres iiij^d."

1531-3. "Two staves for the passion cloth, iiij^d."

1552. *London. St. Nicholas, Cole Abbey.*
"A passion banner of red sarsnet and several others."

1555. *London. St. Peter Cheap.*
"*Item*, payd for ij yards of clothe to make ij passions banners."

1551. (3 Henry VIII.) London. St. Margaret Pattens.
"*Item*, twoo Banner Clothes of the passhion steyned for lent."

1454. *Bristol. St. Ewen* (destroyed). (Churchwardens' Account.)
"*Item*, ij banars of the Passion for lent."

N.B.—The Processional Cross in Lent and Passiontide should not be covered or enveloped in any veil.

Palm Sunday.

"THE devout ceremonies of Palm Sundays in Processions," says *Canon Roger Edgeworth*, of Salisbury, in the time of Henry VIII.,* "and on *Good* Fridays about the laying of the *C*ross and Sacrament into the Sepulchre, gloriously arrayed, be so necessary to succour the capability of man's remembrance, that if they were not used once every year, it is to be feared that *C*hrist's Passion would soon be forgotten." To this *Fuller* adds that it was done "in memory of the receiving of *C*hrist into Hierusalem, a little before His death, and that we may have the same desire to receive Him into our hearts"

Dominica in Palmis was known under a variety of names—Branch Sunday, Olive Sunday, Sallow or Willow Sunday, or the Sunday of the Willow Boughs, Yew Sunday, Fig Sunday, Pascha Floridum or the "*E*aster of Flowers,"— all taken from the custom of the yew, box or

---

* *Sermons*, fol. 94. (ed. 1557.)

willow-bearing (in lieu of Palm) upon this day in commemoration of the triumphal Entry of our Lord into Jerusalem previous to His Passion.

This custom of palm bearing was without doubt derived from the Jews, who at the feast of Tabernacles were wont to walk every day round the altar with palm branches with sprigs of willow and maple tied to the lower part,* in their hands, singing Hosanna (Save us we pray), whilst one of the priests chanted the Hallel, consisting of Psalms cxiii.-cxviii., the multitudes joining in the responses at certain intervals, waving their branches of willow or palm, shouting as they waved them, "Alleluia," or "Hosanna," or "O Lord, I beseech Thee send now prosperity. (Ps. cxviii. 25). During the ceremony the trumpets sounded on all sides. This ceremony was gone through every morning during the seven days of the festival, and on the seventh day they went seven times round the altar, and this was called the "Great Hosannah," for on this day they used to repeat the Hosannah after, saying, "For thy sake, O our Creator, Hosannah: For thy sake, O our redeemer,

---

* The Palm was grasped in the right hand and a sprig of citron in the left, both being held close together while a benediction expressive of the ceremony was pronounced, the branch being gently shaken. Every congregation was bound to provide them for worshippers.

Hosannah': For thy sake, O our seeker, Hosannah.'' (See the *Jewish Rituals*.)

Heathen conquerors also bore palm trees in their hands.* Those who had conquered in the *Grecian* combats had not only crowns of the palm trees given them, but carried branches in their hands.† The Romans did the same in their triumphs and they sometimes wore the *toga palmata*, a garment interwoven with the figures of palm trees. Moreover, it was usual in the *East* to strew flowers and branches of trees in the way of conquerors, of princes, and of noble persons. Thus we find those esteeming *Christ* as the Messiah and their King acting in a similar way towards Him. *Herodotus*‡ gives a like instance when the people went before Xerxes passing over the Hellespont, burning all manner of perfumes on the bridges, and strewing the way with myrtles. The employment of boughs and hymns were usual among the *Grecians* on all festivals *(Clemens ex Orpheo)*. Thus Athenian feasts were named τα οσχοφορια *(Grotius)*. According to *Tacitus* flowers were strewn

---

* A. Gell, *Noct. Att.*, liii. c. 6.

† ALEX. ab. Alex. *Genial Dier.* lv. c. 8.

‡ (vii. p. 404.)

before Nero on his return from the Grecian Games.*

This procession of palms is of very early date, the *E*astern Church having observed it as far back as the fourth century. Branches of the palm tree were by no means used exclusively for the ceremony, especially here in England where box, willow, yew, and other evergreen boughs were brought largely into requisition, real palm in any quantity being unattainable. In the *Sarum* mass book neither palms nor olives are specified in the rubrics, the ceremony being called *benedictio florum et frondium* merely. It is not quite clear what the flowers were which are thus ordered to be blessed, whether the flowers of the willow or "boxfloures," or flowers to be strewn in the procession, or the decoration of the church-yard cross. "Here *C*ryst passyth forth, ther metyth with hym serteyn of chylderyn with flowres, and cast beforn hym, and they synggyn 'Gloria Laus.'"—Christ's *E*ntry in Jerusalem. *Coventry Miracle Play.* At any rate "flowers" are frequently mentioned in the entries under Palm Sunday in the old parish accounts:

---

* *Ann.* Appendix by *Murphy*, l. 16. 12. See also SUETONIUS, s. 25. Vid ADAMI *Observat*, p. 150. ALTMANNO *Obs.* Vol. II., p. 420. J. LYDIUS in *Agonist Sacr.*, p. m. 152, and KUINOEL *Comment.*, Vol. I., p. 528.

1396-7. *Abingdon Abbey.* (Sacristan's Account.)

" In frondibus die Palmarum xj^d."

17-19. *Edward IV. London St. Mary-at-Hill.* (Churchwardens' Accounts.)

" Palm, box, cakes and flowers, Palm Sunday Eve, viij^d."

1486. " *Item*, for flowers, obleyes, and for box and palm agendt Palm Sunday, vj^d."

1510. *London. St. Martin, Outwich.* (Churchwardens' Accounts.)

" Paid for palme, boxfloures, and cakes, iiij^d."

" Paid for kaks, flowers, and yow, ij^d."*

1511-12. *London. St. Andrew, East Cheap.* (Churchwardens' Accounts.)

" *Item*, payd for palme and yew palme sondaye, iv^d."

" *Item*, payd for wyne, Cakes and floures vj^d."

1516. " *Item*, payd for palym & fflowers & kakys, v^d."

1517. " *Item*, paide ffor palme & box & bred, iv^d. ob."

---

* Neale. *Views of most interesting Churches*, ii. p. 13.

> 1520-1. "*Item*, paid for palme, ewe &
> Box and cakes, v$^{d.}$ ob."
>
> 1556. (4. Mary.) *London. St. Michael,
> Cornhill.* (Churchwardens' Accounts.)
> "*Item*, paide for palme, box, yew, flowers
> and cakes for Palme Sondaie, viij$^{d.}$ ob."
>
> 1565. (7. *Eliz.*) *London. St. Peter Cheap.*
> "paid to Sexton for hearbes on Palm
> Sunday, ij$^{d.}$"

The Salisbury benediction rubric says the
"flowers and palms" were presented on the
altar "for the clergy," and at *Ghent* the bishop
still carries a nosegay of various flowers on
Palm Sunday.* The cakes, obleyes, and bread
so frequently alluded to in these old accounts
were "singing cakes" or unconsecrated wafers
which were thrown down together with the
flowers amongst the singing boys during
the procession. "The procession came,"
says a seventeenth century (*circa* 1600) writer
describing some ceremonial observances during
Queen Mary's reign, "with the Blessed
Sacrament and with a little bell ringing and
singing . . . and coming near the Porch a
boy or one of the Clerks, did cast over among

---

* *Cæremoniale Episcoporum* (ii. 21) suggests that if true palms
cannot be had, little flowers or crosses of palm should be attached
to the olive boughs.

the boys, flowers and singing cakes."* Wafer
bread used for the Mass was commonly called
" singing bread," or " singing cakes," or
" housling bread," because used in singing
mass, but this kind of bread was also used
at the same time as other confectionery. The
wine was for the use of the Singers of the
Passion.

It has been thought by some that the yew-
tree (one or two of which were customarily
planted in old churchyards) was so cultivated
with the very object that its branches might
be used in these Palm Sunday processions.
An old Sermon for " *Dominica in Ramis
Palmarum* " would seem to support this
contention :

> " For encheson we have non oliffe that
> bereth grene leues we taken in stede of it
> hew and palmes wyth, and beroth abowte
> in procession, and so this day we callyn
> palme Sonnenday."—Hampson's *Medii
> Ævi Kal. Book IV. p.* 300.

Yew is still called " palm " in many places,—
just as the *willow* is so called in the North of
England, Scotland and Germany to-day,—in
consequence of its ancient use on this day—
" Palme the yelowe that groweth on wyllowes."

---

* Neale. *Views of Most Interesting Churches*, vol. ii.

In *Russia* this day is called "Sallow Sunday" from the necessary employment of *sallows* in the procession.

In the extended version of the Hymn *Gloria Laus* by its probable author Theodulphus, Bishop of Orleans (p. 821), there is a clear reference to the use of willow branches in the procession:

Castaque pro ramis salicis præcordia sunto
Nos operum ducat prata ad amœna viror.

Barnaby Goodge, in the *Popish Kingdom*, published 1570, alludes to the use of willow branches at that time instead of palm.

In 1709 the churchwardens of *St. Dunstan's, Canterbury*, caused a "palm tree" to be planted in their churchyard, and which could have been none other than a yew tree, a theory borne out by an entry in the church accounts of *Woodbury, Devonshire*, where in 1775 "a yew or palm tree was planted in churchyard ye south side of the church, in the same place where one was blown down by the wind a few years ago."

The *Cloister Garth* at Wells was called Palm Churchyard perhaps for a similar reason.

Other authorities contradict this by asserting that the ascribed funereal nature of the tree forbade its use in joyful solemnities. In the reign of Edward IV., about 1470, yew trees were ordered to be cultivated in churchyards to supply the yeomanry with bows. Thus the "shooter ewe" is alluded to by Chaucer, in the "*Assembly of Foules,*" and "yew, of which bows are made," by Spencer in his "*Faerie Queene.*" In the time of William III. a sprig of yew was worn in the cap as a sign of mourning and also stuck about the winding sheets of the dead, but the wearing of the *willow* was a much more general sign of mourning, yet we have seen that that did not prevent its use on Palm Sunday.* Evergreens were ever symbols of life, but according to their drooping character a funereal significance has been attached to them. The yew is such a tree with its roots among the dead, rising pregnant with life and victory over the grave, and from its great strength and durability of life a fitting symbol of the resurrection.†

The *Pontifical of Egbert,* Archbishop of York (732-766), contains probably the earliest known

---

* What means . . . this mournynge looke, this Vesture sad, this wrethe of Wyllow-tree . . ?" Eglog Sexta, p. 251. Goodge, *Eglogs, Epytaphes* and *Sonnettes.* "My Phillida is dead! I'll stick a branch of willow at my fair Phillis' head." Corydon's Doleful Knell. *Percy Reliques,* p. 246. The Cypress was used by Pagans for funerals and mourning. Yew was associated at a very early date with ideas of sorrow and immortality. The Egyptians used it as a symbol of mourning, and the Greeks, Romans and early Britons.

† Yew used for Palm Sunday. See *Gentleman's Magazine,* vol. i., p. 128. Boys of Lanark Grammar School, according to ancient usage, used to parade streets with a large tree of the willow kind, *salix cafrea,* in blossom, ornamented with daffodils, mezereon, and box tree. Day there called *Palm Saturday.*

form of blessing the palms.* The Sarum form of benediction differs from that of the Roman and other Missals; the Procession and Stations, however, have some similitude The office consists of three portions—the Benediction of Palms, the Procession with the same, and the Mass. At *Salisbury* the blessing was made on the third step, the flowers and palms were presented on the altar for the clergy, for others on the stair only. They were it seems laid upon a cushion:

> 1450. *Bristol, St. Ewen* (destroyed).
> (Churchwardens' Accounts.)
> "*Item*, one Coshyn for Palm Sonda."

The blessing over the distribution took place, first to the clergy and others in quire, then to the men and afterwards to the women of the congregation, all of whom took part in the annual procession: antiphons being sung meanwhile.†

It is impossible to say how far the ritual practised at Sarum Cathedral was adopted in parish churches,—(for of old every village church in England had its procession of palms on this day)—but of necessity it must have been generally in an extremely modified form. The Palm Sunday rite at Sarum was a magnificent and imposing ceremony, especially the procession.

---

* Surtees Society, pp. 128, 135–6.

† The Processions were arranged in the Porch on Palm Sunday, Holy Cross Day, and Rogations.

The following is a synopsis of the Stations:

	Sarum Cathedral.	Parish Churches. i.	Parish Churches. ii.
Benediction of Palms. Procession.	High Altar. West ... od. Cl ... Canons' ... in East Walk of ...	High Altar. West Quire ... North Dr.	... Al. Quire gate.
First Station.	At the end of the Laics' Cemetery (Eastern?) north of the ... Here it was met by the Shrine with the ...	Eas[t] end of Church.	... behind altar by the North or o[f] the S. ... Behind of South
Second Station.	South side of Church. East of Cloisters.	Sou[t]h s[i]de	Middle of South aisle.
Third Station.	North walk of ...	Wes[t] (or South ... od.	Wes[t] ed.
Fourth Station.	West d[o]or of Church. Enter the ... Before he Rood (wh[i]ch is th[e]n ...	West Quire ...	Quire Ga[t]e.

All having entered the Quire, all crosses throughout the church are uncovered and remain so until after *E*vensong :

> 1540. (27 Henry VIII,) *Ludlow.* (Churchwardens' Accounts.)
>
> " *Item*, payd for ij cordes to drawe up the clothe afore the rode on Palm Sondaye, ij^d."
>
> 1557. " *Item*, for hangynge the clothe over the roode upon Palme Sonday, and the locker for drawing the same vj^d."
>
> " They also, upon Palmes Sonday, life up a cloth, and say hayle our Kynge ! to a rood made of a wooden blocke."*
>
> " On Palme Sondaye at procession the priest draweth up the veyle before the rode, and falleth down to the ground with all the people, and saith twice, Ave Rex Noster, Hayle be thou our King."†
>
> On this day all crosses remain uncovered till after *E*vensong : " Omnes cruces per Ecclesiam suit discoopertæ usque post vesperas."—*Missale Sarum*, p. 262.

At places other than Salisbury the course of the procession differed considerably, *e.g.*, at *Evesham Abbey*, where the Stations were but

---

* *A short description of Antichrist*, fol. 26.
† *Ibid.* p. 15b.

three, *i.e.* (i) on Merstow Green ; (ii) before the Church doors (West ?), after passing through the High Street by the Cemetery Gate ; (iii) " as in solemn processions" before the *Great Rood.* In the event of unfavourable weather the procession made a circuit of the Cloister, in which case the Stations were : *a,* Chapter House (*E*ast) ; *b,* School (on the Guest-house side) (West) ; *c,* to the Church as above. The Second Station in parish churches appears to have been generally made in the cemetery or churchyard, at the Cross. By the *Constitutions of William* (de Bleys), Bishop of Worcester (1229), a cross decent and handsome was to be erected in the cemetery or churchyard, to which processions might be made on Palm Sunday, unless otherwise accustomed.

> " *De Cemeterio.* In ornatu coemeterii ipsum coemeterium sit decenter circumvallatum muro vel sepe, vel fossato ; nulla pars coemeterii aedificiis occupata sit, nisi tempore hostilitatis. Crux decens et honesta, vel in ipso coemeterio erecta, ad quam fiet processio ipso die Palmarum, nisi in alio loco consuvit fieri."
> —Wilkins' *Concilia,* i. 623.

The old parish books of *St. Andrew Hubbard* have an entry for the year 1524-5 : " To James

Walker, for making clene the Churchyard ag'st Palm Sunday, 1d."

Henry Brown by his Will dated 1501, made provision for a cross to be set up in Hardley Churchyard "*pro palmis in die Ramis Palmarum offerendis.*"*

This churchyard cross was known in some places as the "palm cross," *crux buxata* (from *buxus*—box), and took the form of a stone crucifix near the south entrance of the church; and which was decorated on Palm Sunday with flowers and palm branches.†

The procession as it occurred in parish churches is described by *Clement Maideston*, an old commentator on the Sarum rite. Dr. Rock in his *Church of Our Fathers* (Vol. iii. part ii. pp. 227-89) gives it, but not verbatim:

" While they were going from the north side towards the east, and had just ended the Gospel read at the first station, the shrine with the Sacrament, surrounded with lights in lanterns and streaming banners, and preceded

---

* Blomefield's, *Norfolk* (x. 141). See *Rock*, iii. 228. "De aliis cæremoniis hujus processionis faciendis, tam quæ vulfariter Appellatur Crux Osannere."—Ordinarium MS. S. Petri Areævall ap Ducange.

† It is still the custom in some places to adorn the graves with flowers upon this day, a remnant probably of this old ceremonial. In some parts of Wales laurel leaves plastered over with gold leaf were used with a probable like connection.

by a silver cross and a thurifer with incense, was borne forwards so that they might meet it as it were, and our Lord was hailed by the singers chanting, *Ecce rex venit mansuetas.* Kneeling lowly down and kissing the ground they saluted the Sacrament again and again in many appropriate sentences out of Holy Writ; and the red wooden cross withdrew from the presence of the silver crucifix. The whole procession now moved to the south side of the close or churchyard, where, in cathedrals, a temporary erection was made for the boys who sang the *Gloria, laus,* as a halt was made for a Second Station."

"From the stone cross, . . . the procession went next to the western doorway, if the church had one, otherwise to the south porch, and there paused to make its Third Station. The door itself was shut, but after awhile flew wide open. The priests who bore the shrine with the Blessed Sacrament and relics, stepped forwards with the heavenly burden, and held it up on high at the doorway, so that all that went in had to go under this shrine; and thus the procession came back into church, each one bowing his head as he passed beneath the Sacrament."

Roger Martin, who died in 1580, gives the

following description of the Palm Sunday ceremonies as they occurred in his youth in *Melford Parish Church, Suffolk:*

"Upon Palm Sunday, the Blessed Sacrament was carried in procession about the churchyard, under a fair canopy, borne by four yeomen. The procession coming to the church gate went westward, and they with the Blessed Sacrament went eastward; and when the procession came against the door of Mr. Clopton's aisle, they, with the Blessed Sacrament and with a little bell and singing, approached at the east end of our Lady's Chapel; at which time a boy with a thing in his hand pointed to it, signifying a prophet, as I think, and sang, standing upon the turret that is on the said Mr. Clopton's aisle door: *Ecce Rex tuus venit,* etc. And then all did kneel down, and then rising up, went singing together into the church, and coming near the porch, a boy or one of the clerks did cast over among the boys flowers and singing cakes."*

That the Blessed Sacrament was customarily borne in the Palm Sunday procession is amply upheld by the testimony of ancient wills, church inventories, etc., thus we find *Robert Thurston,* of Mekyll Waldyngfield, in 1494,

---

* Neale. *Views of most interesting Churches,* vol.

directing his executors to " provyde and ordeyn
a clenly seler [*selour* or " celour,"—a canopy
with back and side curtains] for to be born
ouyr the sacrament on Palme Sunday and on
Corpus Xti. Day." In 1552 (6. Edward VI.)
at *Moulsford, Berks.*, was a " canabe for palme-
sondaye of grene and Red satene"; at *St.
Mary, Bletchingley, Surrey*, " a clothe that was
wonte to be borne on Palme Sunday."*

From the earliest times in *E*ngland there
seems to have been a procession on Palm
Sunday in commemoration of the triumphal
entry of our Lord into Jerusalem. In the
seventh century *St. Aldhelm* (*De Laude Virg.*,
cap. 15.) declares it to have been done on
ancient authority, and *Alcuin* in the following
century further tells us that the Holy *G*ospel
was carried on a shrine or feretory during this
procession. The introduction of the Blessed
Sacrament into the Palm Sunday procession
is generally ascribed to *Lanfranc*, who when
Abbot of Bec ordered a like ceremony, and
one which was particularly confined to *E*ngland
and Normandy; and " although," says Mr.
Edmund Bishop,[1] " the observance is in fact

---

* The *Ludlow* Church Accounts for 1555-7 have charges for " pyns
and poynts to dresse the canapie to beare over the sacrament on Palme
Sondaye," and for " pyns and poynts upon Palme Soudaye, to tye up
the coverelett in the churche over the offrynge place."

[1] "*Holy Week
Rites of
Sarum,
Herford,
and Rouen
compared.*"
Tr. S. S.
Osmund., vi.,
part iv. p. 100.

prescribed in Lanfranc's statutes for Canterbury Cathedral (which in the twelfth and thirteenth centuries were known as "the Bec Customs"), and is not mentioned by John of Avranches, the question is not at all an easy one to settle, and the difficulties are considerable either way. If anything, the probabilities may perhaps be that the custom arose rather in *England.*"

It is on the authority of *Matthew of Paris* that the introduction is accredited to Lanfranc, for he says that the directory, which had been drawn up by the latter for the Abbey of Bec, was soon adopted in the larger Benedictine Abbeys in *England.* Lanfranc's directions are as follows :[1]

Opera franci,"
Giles,
o.

"After tierce the abbot blesses the palms and flowers. The palms are carried by the abbot and other dignitaries, branches and flowers by the rest. All the bells are rung while the procession leaves the choir. Servants lead the way with the banners, then a lay brother with holy water, two others with crosses, and two with candlesticks and lighted tapers, two with thuribles. Then two subdeacons carrying two books of the *Gospels,* followed by the lay monks. Next the boys with their masters, then the rest of the brethren two and two, and lastly the abbot." Antiphons

were sung during the progress of the procession. The *Directory* continues: "A little
before daybreak a place had been prepared,
to which the body of our Lord had been carried
by two priests and placed in a shrine. When
the procession reaches this place it halts, and
the two priests vested in white come forward.
The banner and cross-bearers having moved
forward, the two priests take up the feretory
with the Body of Christ and stand still." "The
procession is ranged around and antiphons
are sung, at the end of each of which they
genuflect. When the abbot intones the antiphon *Ave Rex noster*, the bearers of the feretory
go forward, preceded by the banners and
crosses, and pass up between the lines of the
rest of the procession. As the Blessed
Sacrament passes they genuflect two and two.
Then they follow in procession till they reach
the gates of the city, where a halt or station
is made, and the feretory is laid on a table
covered with a pall, in the entrance to the
gates. The gateway is adorned with curtains
and rich hangings." "The boys sing the
Gloria, Laus, and other antiphons, and at the
Ingrediente Domino the procession returns, the
great bells of the city ringing during the rest of
the procession. When the procession returning

comes to the gates of the monastery another Station is made before a temporary altar. Antiphons are sung. The Blessed Sacrament is again taken up, and they enter the Church, and make the third Station before the crucifix uncovered for the purpose. Then the Mass begins."

Among the magnificent gifts of *Simon*, nineteenth *Abbot of St. Alban's*, in the latter part of the twelfth century, was a splendid shrine for carrying the Host in the Palm Sunday procession, which Matthew Paris calls " *Vas mirificum.*" He decreed that this shrine bearing the Body of Christ should be carried by a brother venerable for character as well as for age, clothed in a white chasuble, to a pavilion erected in the churchyard and composed of the most precious stuffs, unless inclemency of weather should prevent. Thence it was carried to the Chapter House and then back to the Church with the greatest veneration.

At *Chichester* the Eucharist was also carried in a shrine-shaped vessel by an old monk in a white chasuble supported by two others in copes, to a tent prepared in the cemetery, thence to the Chapter House, and back into the church, while at *Durham* it would appear that the portable Easter Sepulchre was so used and appeared in sight of the multitude just as the words *Benedictus quo venit*, etc., at the close of the Gospel were being said, and on reaching the Station the Holy Sacrament was incensed and adored.

The *Sarum Missal* directs a shrine with relics in which was to hang a pyx with the Host to be made ready while the distribution of palms was in progress, which preceded by a lantern with an unveiled cross and two banners was to meet the procession at the place of the first Station, the ministers in apparelled albes and amices without tunicles, the priest in a red cope. Very similar are the directions in the *York Missal.** Here a silver (white) cope is prescribed, and the Officiant (after the arrival of the procession) genuflecting to our Lord three times, saying: *Dignus es, Domine Deus noster, accipere gloriam et honorem*, " Thou art worthy, O Lord our God, to receive glory and honour," the choir following his example each time with the same words. After which the Blessed Sacrament was carried back to the church by another way. This ceremony was performed without the church, weather permitting, where the Host was placed under a tent (*tentorium*).

---

* *Surtees Soc.* (1874), p. 86.

The weather being unpropitious the Eucharist was honoured upon the Lady Altar.

The *unveiled* cross was to lead the procession,* and lights in lanterns were to precede the Eucharist. The MS. Inventory of *St. Peter's, Cornhill,* has " a lantern of horn for Palm Sonday," and that of *St. Dunstan in the East* a similar entry. Lanfranc's *Constitutions* thus refer to it :†

> " Accendatur Cereus quem portare in
> hastâ debet Secretarius, accendatur et
> candela in laterna hanc portare debet
> unus de magistris puerorum,"

while that at Canterbury is described " hasta ad portandum cereum ad novum ignem."‡

Naogeorgus says that a wooden ass bearing a figure of Christ was borne upon wheels through the streets to the church door, where the priest blessed the palms as talismans against storms and lightning, and then lay down before it, and was beaten with a rod by another priest! Two " lubborers " then

---

* An old writer observes " They have their laudable dumme ceremonies, with Lentin Crosse and Uptide Crosse, and these two must jostle til lent break his necke. Then cakes must be caste out of the steple, that al the boyes in the parish must lie scrambling together by the eares, tyl all the parish falleth a laughyng."

† Wilkins' *Concilia* i. 339.

‡ Dart. *Appen.* xii.

alluded to the entry of our Lord into Jerusalem, and the ass smothered with branches was drawn into the church. A remnant of this may perhaps have been seen in the custom once prevailing on Palm Sundays at *Caistor Church, Lincolnshire*, where a whip, to which was tied a purse containing thirty pieces of silver, and to which four twigs of witch elm were fastened, were offered during the service. A gad (goad) whip was used in connection with the wooden ass.

THE PROPHET.—The introduction of the Prophet—"an acolyte in the guise of a prophet"*—to sing the *Prophetic Lesson* after the *Gospel* at the first Station of the procession, though no part of the rite and interesting only as a survival of the ancient liturgical drama, seems to have been very generally adopted not only in cathedral, but also in parish churches. It appeared in Mr. Roger Martin's account of Palm Sunday in Melford Parish Church, Suffolk, as well as in the Cathedral Church of Sarum. Many of our old parish accounts bear witness to the like usage:

1451. *London. St. Mary at Hill.* (Churchwardens' Accounts.)

---

* Sarum *Processionale*, pp. 50-51.

"Payd to Loreman for playing the p'phet on Palm Sunday, iiij^{d.}"

1519. *London. St. Peter Cheap.*

"*Item*, for hyering of the heres for the p'fetys uppon Palme Sondaye, xij^{d.}"

1531. (17-19 *Edward IV.*) *London. St. Mary at Hill.*

"Pd. for the hire of the rayment for the Prophets, xij^{d.}, and of Cloth of Arras, js. iiij^{d.}, for Palm Sonday."

In 1520 the churchwardens of *St. Andrew Hubbard's* paid 8d. "for the hire of an angel"; in 1535-7 a similar sum for "a Preest and chylde that playde a messenger," and an angel is hired for 4d., while the wardens of *All Hallows, Staining*, pay eight pence for "the hiring of a pair of wings and a crest for an angel." The churchwardens of *St. Peter Cheap* in their accounts for 1534 make the entry: "*Item*, p'd for the settyng up of the stages for the prophets on Palm Sonday and for nayllys, iiij^{d.}"

In the *Sarum Missal* the antiphon "Gloria, and honour, and laud be to Thee, King Christ the Redeemer,"* etc., is directed to be sung by seven boys *in loco eminentiore*

---

* Composed by Theodulph, an Italian bishop of Orleans, in the prison of Angers, in 835.

(in a prominent place). At *Winchester*, *Chichester* and other Cathedrals, the gallery over the west Porch was used by the singers on Palm Sunday. Similar galleries exist in some Parish Churches as at *Weston-in-Gordano*, *Somerset*, where a remnant of a small gallery remains over the south door, within the Porch, approached by narrow stone stairs. Above the porch door at Wraxall Church, in the same county, is a similar gallery. The general custom, however, seems to have been to utilise the Rood Loft for the purpose, or a temporary erection set up for the occasion.

On the exterior of the West front of churches, over a porch there is frequently a gallery, in which the choir sang (as in English mediæval cathedrals, and as now at Lisieux) the "Gloria, Laus," as the procession returned from the cemetery, or at the reception of a bishop. At Albi the boys sang and responded on the Cathedral battlements. In the case of in-clement weather it would probably be sung before the altar of the cross in the rood loft, and which indeed may have led to the con-struction of the inner west gallery. The actors in the mystery plays also used a scaffold built over the church porch, with the inside of the church representing heaven out of which the

Deity came. Frequent charges in reference to such a scaffold in and out of church for such plays are found in old parish accounts. The following are a few concerning the scaffold for Palm Sunday :—

1480-2. *London. St. Andrew Hubbard, East Cheap.*

"*Item*, paid for a frame and workmanshippe over the chirch dore for palm sundaye, vij^{d.}"

1492-3. "*Item*, paid for a leddyr for the chirche porche on palme sonday, x^{d.}"

1493. *London. St. Mary at Hill.*

"For setting up the frame over the porch on Palm Sonday Eve, vj^{d.}"

1521. *London. St. Peter Cheap.*

"*Item*, for nayls for ye frame on the churche dore, j^{d.}"

"*Item*, for lathe & naylys for the skafolde, ij^{d.}"

1525. "Palme Sondaye. *Item*, for lathe naylles & hooks for the pageants and for settyng up of the same, x^{d.}"

1529. "*Item*, payd for bowes fflowrys caaks & for pynnys for lathys & for makyng of the fframys on palme sondaye, ij^{d.}"

1467. *London. St. Michael's, Cornhill.*

"*Item*, payd for nails to tak up the clothes on Palme Sonday."

Anciently the entry into the church at the close of the procession the priest, not the cross-bearer, smote the door with the lower end of the staff of the cross, the door being opened from within. Part of the duties of the subdeacon in those times was to carry the cross in processions.

The Singing of the Passion.—One of the chief features of the Palm Sunday Mass was the solemn chanting of the Gospel for the day or "the Singing of the Passion" as it was called.* An old writer in not too elegant *protestant* language thus refers to it:

" But, lorde, what asses-play they made of it in great cathedral churches and abbies. One comes forth in his albe and his long stole (for so they call their girde that they put about theyr neckes), thys must be leashe wise as hunters weare their hornes. This solempne syre played Christe's part, a God's name. Then another companye of singers, chyldren and al, song, in prick-song, the Jewe's part—

---

* The Passion, according to *St. Matthew*, on Sunday; that of *St. Mark* on Tuesday; of *St. Luke* on Wednesday; and of *St. John* on Good Friday.

and the Deacon read the middel text. The Prest at the alter al this while, because it was tediouse to be unoccupyed, made Crosses of Palme to set upon your doors, and to beare in your pursces to chase away the Divel."

The clergy at *Wells Cathedral* were directed to wear red vestments on Palm Sunday, except a black cope "ad opus Caiaphæ" (*i.e.* for him who takes the part of Caiaphus in the Passion).

This singing of the *Stories of the Passion* on four of the days of the Holy Week was in all probability a remnant of the Mystery Play, and took the place of the ordinary sequence or initial. They were sung in three tones— the deep, the middle, and the exalted. The words or sayings of the Jews or the disciples and others being sung in the exalted tone (*vox alta*—alto); those of the Saviour in the deep tone (*vox bassa*—bass); the third (*vox media*— mean or tenor) being employed in reciting the narrative of the Evangelist. Where the Latin mass is now sung the contralto is called *ancilla*, because to it are assigned the words of the maid in *St. Mark* xiv. 67, 69, etc. (which go to the alto in the Sarum books); and the choir represent the multitude. In *Graduale*, 1528, fol. 89, five voices are distinguished for the Passion. For the three see Missale, p. 264. In

1618, in the Cathedral of *Albi, Aquitaine,* that portion of the Passion called the "Synagogue" ceased to be chanted "en musique," as was the old custom, by order of Bishop D'Elbène.

At *Evesham* the celebrant at the High Mass on this day held a palm at the singing of the Gospel, while at *Sarum* the taper bearers bore branches of palm in lieu of their Gospel candlesticks.

Numerous entries appear in the Church-wardens' accounts in reference to this singing of the Passion:

1447. *London. St. Peter Cheap.*

"*Item,* payde on Palme Sundaye for brede & wyne to the Reders of ye passion, iij^d."

1505. *Reading. St. Lawrence.*

"*Item,* payed to the clerk for syngyng of the passion on Palm Sonday, in ale, i^d."

1509. "*Item,* payed for a q'rt of bastard, for ye syngers of the Passhyon on Palm Sonday, iiij^d."

1524. "*Item,* for drynk in the roode loft vppon Palme Sonday, j^d."*

"*Item,* payd for a q^{a}rte of bastard for the Passion upon Palme Sunday, iij^d."

---

* From this it would appear the Passion was read at the Great Cross in the Rood Loft. The aforenamed Roger Martin supports this. "On Good Friday," he says, "a Priest, then standing by the Rood (in the Loft), sang *The Passion.*"

1541. "Payd for a quart of malmsey for the clerk on Palme Sonday, iiij[d]."

1515. *Bristol. St. Ewen.* (Destroyed.) A "Pott of wyne`on Palme Sunday, j[d]." (an annual charge).

1. Hen. VIII. *Kingston-on-Thames.* "For ale upon Palme Sonday on syngyng of the Passion, ol. os. 1d."

1557-8. *Bristol. St. John Baptist.* "*Item*, paid to the parson for syngyng the Passion on Palme Sunday, vj[d]."

2. Edward VI. *Bristol, S. Ewen.* "In prymis for Readynge the Passion, j[d]."

1562. *London. St. Michael, Cornhill.* "*Item*, paide to a clerke on Palme Sonday for syngyng, iiij[d]."

"*Item*, paide to two clerkes for singing in the church from Wednesday before Easter to Octave."

King Henry VIII., in spite of his reforming proclivities, declared that the custom of palm-bearing on this day was to be continued and *not* cast away, and in the Proclamation issued in his thirtieth year he enjoins that "on Palme Sunday it shall be declared that bearing Palmes reviveth the memorie of the receivinge of Christ in like manere into Jerusalem before

His Deathe." According to *Stow*, in the week before Easter, there were great shows in London for going to the woods, and fetching into the King's house a twisted tree, or withe; and the like into the house of every man of note or consequence. Indeed, so great a hold had this palm-bearing upon the people that it became a proverbial saying that, " He that hath not a palm in his hand on Palm Sunday, must have his hand cut off." By an Act of Common Council, 1 and 2, Philip and Mary, for retrenching expenses, it was ordered "that from henceforth there shall be no wythe fetcht home at the Maior's or Sheriff's houses."

Palms continued to be borne in England until nearly the end of the reign of Edward VI.*

---

* See Dixon's *Church Hist.* ii. pp. 431–91.

Tenebræ.

ON the evenings of Wednesday, Thursday and Friday in Holy Week, the Office called *Tenebræ* was anciently sung in the Church. The name of the Office has been traced to the fact that it was formerly celebrated at midnight, as an allusion to Christ walking no more openly with the Jews, as *Cranmer* says; others suggest it is derived from the gradual extinction of the lights, originally put out one by one as the morning began to grow clear, for *St. Gregory of Tours* says that in the night of Good Friday the watchings were kept in darkness until the third hour, when a small light appeared above the altar; or in symbol of grief and mourning; or as *Beleth* suggests, of the eclipse of three hours at the Passion, and of the desolation and abandonment endured by Christ in His Passion, and the total deprivation of the Jews of the light of the faith when they put our Saviour to death.

The office of *Tenebræ*, consisting as it does of Nocturns, Mattins and Lauds, is essentially a night office—in fact the night offices for the last three days of Holy Week. In primitive times Christians were wont to spend the greater portions of these Holy Week nights in watchings in the churches, when this Office was said at midnight,—a practice universal in the twelfth century—as it still is with the religious orders [1] The Church, however, recognizing that, according to the exigencies of modern times, such an arrangement would be inconvenient, and anxious that her children should not lose so spiritual an aid in so solemn a season, has permitted these offices to be sung—by anticipation, as it were—*i.e.*, on the evening of the day previous, in order that they may participate.

According to the rubric in the *Sarum Breviary* twenty-four candles are lighted at the beginning of the service, but no mention is made there of any stand for them, nor where they are to be placed. The *Synod of Exeter*, however, held under Bishop Peter Quivil, in 1287, declared that every parish church ought to have (among the things mentioned for the parishioners to provide*) a " hercia," " ad

[1] Tenebræ in fact the last lingeri remnant of *Agapæ*, wl was celebrٳ every eveni followed by prophecies Psalms, an instruction after midni; and then t Eucharist. See *Lovin Cup.*

---

* The parishioners by Canon Law are to provide the triangular candlestick to support these candles. (Wilkins, *Concilia*, ii. 139.)

tenebras." In the *Spicileg Fontanell MS.*, p. 394, appears the following : " On Thursday in Holy Week, Good Friday and Holy Saturday, there ought to be a Herse-light at the *right* side of the High Altar, and twenty-six candles on it," and in *Du Cange :* " Candelabrum Ecclesiasticum in modum occæ, seu trigoni confectum nostris Herce — Candelabrum in herciæ modum confectum luminibus variis in-structum, quod ad cenatophii caput erigi solet."

This *Tenebræ* candlestick, called " *Herse* " or " *Hersa* "* in English Cathedral statutes, is a large triangular candelabrum or candlestick, or hearse of brass, latten or iron, upon which the tapers used in the " Tenebræ " Office are set, and which is placed on the epistle or south side of the Sanctuary and altar. It is found mentioned under various names as the " Lenten Hearse," the "Herse Light," as in 1561 at *Ripingale, Lincolnshire,* the " Sepulchre and herse lights " are mentioned as being burned.†
Calfhill says that in England it was called the Judas or Judas Cross. In many instances it probably was constructed of wood ; elder-wood

---

* The word Hearse (Latin, *Hercia*) is derived through the French, *Herse*, a harrow, from *Hericius, Ericius, Ericeus,* or *Eritius,* a hedge-hog.

† Peacock. *English Church Furniture.*

being much used of old during the Easter ceremonies. At *Seville*, entre-los-Coras is a tenebrario of bronze, twenty-five feet in height, made in 1562. The Parish Accounts of St. Michael, Cornhill, for the year 1554 have an entry : " *Item*, paide for makynge of a cross for Judas Candles."

The Tenebræ candles or tapers were sometimes of yellow* (unbleached) wax, save one which was of white (bleached) wax, and corresponded to the number of the twelve prophets and twelve apostles, the white one being representative of our Lord. During the saying or singing of the office they were extinguished one by one at the beginning of each Antiphon and Responsory, since the number of candles and of Antiphons and Responsories in the History are equal and signify the cruelty of the Jews as recorded in the Prophets and Apostles · the last remaining (the white one) being hidden away lighted, generally behind the altar, after the last Psalm. In some cases the lights were extinguished at once or at two or three intervals; in others they were quenched with a moist sponge, and in others with a hand of wax, to represent Judas. Yet about the year 840, *Theodore*, archdeacon of Rome, told Amalarius

---

* Pale yellow in the dress of Judas, signified deceit.

that the lights were not extinguished on Maundy Thursday in St. John's Lateran.

The Tenebræ Candles, besides prefiguring our Lord and His Apostles—who fled from Him at His betrayal,—are variously interpreted to represent the patriarchs and prophets whose light was dark to the infidel Jews; the light of faith preached by the Apostles and their Divine Master, of which faith the fundamental witness is the Mystery of the Blessed Trinity (symbolized by the triangular herse), while the upper light, called sometimes the Lady Candle, is said to represent the Blessed Virgin who remained constant, while all the rest, representing the Apostles, had been extinguished one by one. *Sir Thomas More* says the single candle left burning symbolized St. Mary standing beneath the Cross of Calvary; while by others it was more generally regarded as representative of the True Light Himself.

"On these three days," says *Honorius Gallus*, "we celebrate the burial of our Lord; but the three days and nights we reckon for seventy-two hours. And therefore we extinguish so many lights because we mourn the True Light extinguished on these days, and express the sorrow of the seventy-two disciples, which they had on account of the setting of the Eternal

Day and the Sun of Justice, whose hours they were. For these hours, to wit, from the sixth to the ninth, there was darkness when Christ hung on the cross. These three hours we represent by the three nights, which we observe by the extinction of the lights. By the day illumined by the sun, Christ; by the night illumined by the moon, the present Church; by the twelve hours of the day or night, the twelve apostles are signified, because therefrom the hours of the day and night are twenty-four, and on fast days twenty-four *Gloria Patries* are sung, therefore the twenty-four lights are illuminated on these nights, which we distinguish at each canticum, because, like the Apostles, we mourn the setting of the true Sun."*

Amalarius says the extinction of the lights signified the sorrow in the hearts of the disciples while Christ lay in the Sepulchre; and that they were extinguished when beginning the Chant, that in every article of any unforeseen joy we might be affected with sorrow.†
Rupert adds, "the darkness signified the blindness of the Jews and the darkness of the

---

* *Gemma Animæ*, p. 1279.

† *De Ordine Antiphonarii*, ch. xliv., p. 541.

Crucifixion; the lights, the saints; the extinction, the slaughter of them."*

The upper light is not extinguished, but concealed or hidden, generally behind the altar (another authority says, under the altar, until Easter, which is left in darkness), while the *Miserere* is recited in a low tone, after which it is restored to its place at the top of the candlestick, because God did not leave the Soul of our Lord in hell, nor suffer His Holy One to see corruption, but raised Him from the dead.

In some places, previous to the reinstatement of the candle, a sudden noise with books, or beating on the desks is made at the end of the prayer *Respice*, symbolical of the confusion of the disciples at the betrayal of the Lord, and the convulsion of nature at His death, and as a signal for the bringing forth of the hidden candle and the kindling of all the church lights. At *Florence* and other places the laity joined with discordant and irreverent levity. At *Seville* a volley of musketry customarily is fired.†

---

* L. v. ch. xxvi., p. 953.

† The Jews at the Feast of Purim make a terrible noise in the synagogue at the mention of the name of Hamon: some drum with their feet on the floor, and the boys have mallets with which to knock and make a noise.

The number of candles used in the Tenebræ Office appear to have varied very much in the different churches: the *Sarum Breviary* says twenty-four; at *Canterbury* and *York* there were twenty-five. The *Roman use* orders fifteen, but at *Nevers** there were nine; at *Mans* twelve; at *Paris* and *Rheims* thirteen; at *Cambray* and *St. Quentin* twenty-four; *Evereux* twenty-five; *Amiens* twenty-six; *Coutances* forty-four. In some churches the candles corresponded to each psalm and .lesson of the office; thus we find 7, 9, 12, 15, 24, 30, 72, or as many as each person thought fit to bring.

Frequent reference to the Tenebræ candles are found in mediæval parish accounts, *e.g.*, those of *St. Andrew Hubbard, East Cheap, London.*

> 1525-6. "Payd ffor j^{lb} ½ of tenebræ Candylles & for crosse Candylles x$^{d.}$"

> 1526-7. "Paid ffor iij quarters ½ waste of tenebyr Candelles ffor A crose candell & for garnyschynge of six torches, ij$^{s.}$ x$^{d.}$"

> 1527-8. "Paid for tenebre candelles and Judas candelles, ij$^{d.}$"

---

* Pugin's Glossary.

but it is next to impossible to find anything distinct about them from their, almost without exception, being thrown in with other church wax ; *e.g. :*

> 1555. *St. Michael, Cornhill, London.*
> "Paide for the Paskcull wth the crosse candell, and ij^lis of Tenebar candles weiyinge all vij^lis at xi^d. a pounde vi^s v^d."

At rare intervals an entry such as the following, throws a little more light upon the matter :

> 1493-4. *St. Ewen, Bristol.* (Destroyed.)
> "3 Hondan and 14 crosse tapers,"

but in all probability they differed but little from the common wax tapers in every day use.

The *Tenebræ* Office should be sung without instrumental accompaniment. *Gloria Patri* is not sung According to English usage, the Hebrew Titles were customarily sung in the eleventh century, when the *Constitutions of Lanfranc* mention them as being sung. *Cranmer* explains that the Lamentations of the Prophet Jeremiah were read in memory of the Jews seeking our Lord's life at this time. The Reproaches and Trisagion were not sung on Good Friday until the fourteenth century.

On the three last days of Holy Week, when Ube
Clappers. the bells were not rung, the Clappe, or Clapper—a wooden rattle or trick-track, was used to summon people to church, being used as well in the services in church. This Clapper was known under a variety of names—Crécelle, tarturelle, rattelle, semantron, crotolus—and derived its origin from the Celtic cloc, which preceded the use of bells, a board with knockers. The Greeks used the *hagiosideron* (sacred iron), a mallet and plate of iron, and the *hagia xula* (sacred wood), two clappers as summons to prayer. The latter is mentioned by *John Climacus* as used for rapping at the cell door in monasteries, of Palestine, in the 6th century, as a night signal and waking hammer, as it is to-day in religious houses for a like purpose, and at *University College, Oxford,* where the Fellows are summoned to a meeting in the Common Room by the blow of a hammer at the stair foot. By the *Rule of Pachomius* a trumpet was used.

At *Burgos* the clappers are called matraca; in *Italy* serandola; in some parts of *France* symandres, which sound for service between the Mass on Maundy Thursday, and Gloria in Excelsis, sung on Easter Eve in the Mass after Nones, when the bells are disused in memory of our Lord's silence in the tomb and the speech-less timidity of the Apostles. *Neogeorgus* says that in England boys carried rattles in the procession [of the Host to the Sepulchre] on Good Friday. In 1491 at *Auch* the people were summoned with a horn; the Missal of 1555 says a "trumpet." From Peacock's *Lincolnshire Church Furniture* we find clappes or clappers were burned or otherwise destroyed at the churches of Fullerbie, Mintinge, Skelling-ton and West Reason in the first and second years of the reign of Queen Elizabeth.

Maundy Thursday.

THURSDAY in Holy Week was anciently
known in England as *Sheer,** *Char,* *Shrift,*
or *Shorp Thursday,* a name derived by some
from the public absolution given to penitents
upon this day, by others from the custom of
men polling their heads and beards as a token
of grief for our Lord's betrayal. *John Myre* in
the fourteenth century, thought it to allude
to this hair and beard cutting as a preparation
for Easter. "For that in old Fathers days the
people would that day shear their heads and
clip their beards, and so make them honest
against Easter Day."† Other names for this
day were *Cœna Domini,* the Lord's Supper; or
Feria Quinta in Cœna Domini, so called from
the Mandatum, our Lord's new commandment
of Love (St. John xiii.), through the first

---

* *Sheer,* from the old root *Skier,* signifying pain and affliction. In
the north of England this day is "Kiss Thursday," in allusion to the
kiss of Judas.

† Fllis, quoted by Brand, *Pop. Antiq.*

Antiphon; *Mandatum novum do vobis*, or *Manucando*, from eating the Supper (1 Cor. xi. 24). Its English appellation *Maundy Thursday* comes from the "maund" or basket, from which the gifts were made to the poor at the ceremonial washing of feet: the term "Cœna Domini" being here anciently applied to Ascension Day.*

In mediæval times it was called the Birthday of the Chalice, or the Eucharist, in memory of the institution of the Holy Eucharist. In Austria it was known as *Antlatz-Tag*, Remission Day, from the reconciliation and readmission into the Church of penitents previous to their restoration to communion at Easter.

The chief ancient ceremonies of this day were the Reconciliation of the penitents, put out of the Church on Ash Wednesday, the Consecration of Chrism, the Stripping and Washing of the Altars, and the washing of the feet of the poor in imitation of the washing of the Disciples' feet by our Lord.

As early as the fifth century this day was observed by a celebration and by the washing of the feet of others (lavanda); the usage in *France* and *Africa* being to have an evening

---

* "Quia scilicet mysterium Dominicæ cœnæ a Christo fuit institutum."—*Du Cange.*

celebration, a custom formally abolished by the *Council* of *Constantinople* in 691, as an innovation on Apostolic tradition and discipline.

Lent was the time of solemn penance, anciently enjoined by the bishop alone, and ordinarily restricted to this season, the offender being put out of the church, and reconciliation —(at first restricted to bishops, but at the time of the death of *St. Cyprian* and the *Councils* of *Seville, Agde,* and *Elvira,* power of private reconciliation was given to priests and deacons) —or absolution, given on Maundy Thursday :

> 1505. *Great St. Mary's, Cambridge.*
> "*Item,* vj yernes perteynyng to the shryvyng stole for Lenton."
> 1511. *St. Margaret Pattens, London.*
> "*Item,* a Clothe for lent to hange before the Srevying pewe."

The office of general confessor or penitentiary priests in a diocese, mentioned by *Sozomen* and *Socrates,* was abolished by *Nectarius,* of Constantinople, in the reign of Theodosius, and generally in the East, but it was retained in the West for regulating penance and hearing confessions. Deans and priests of penitents are mentioned by the *Council* of *Agde,* in the ceremonial of Ash Wednesday, as imposing penance on offenders. In England in 1237, as at *Salisbury*, general confessors were appointed in all cathedral churches, and others in every rural deanery were nominated by the bishop to receive confessions from ˅parsons and minor clerks who were reluctant to make them to the rural deans.

In 1281 the reconciliation was made by imposition of hands. In the East public absolution was given on Good Friday or Easter Eve; in the West on Maundy Thursday, and in both churches at the time of Mass, before the Lord's Prayer. The right of public absolution was obtained by priests in the ninth century.

The penitents in hair or sackcloth and ashes (in later penitential times they wore violet), stood before the ambon, from whence the bishop laid his hands upon them, after being entreated by his clergy in set forms of address. Penitents were anciently shorn, as appears from *Paulinus* and the *Third Council* of *Toledo*, a custom censured in the fourth and fifth centuries by *St. Jerome* and Optatus as unbecoming spiritual persons. At *Orleans* the Grand Penitentiary headed a procession of penitents who made the circuit of the choir, singing litanies, on their knees, two and two, with faces veiled, and their bodies clothed in sheets.

In the primitive church three kinds of penance was imposed: (1) segregation, *aphorismos;* prohibition of offering at the altar, for lighter offences; (2) deprivation of communion for faults more grave; (3) effacement of name from the list of the faithful, and exclusion from the church for great sins. At first the deacons interposed, and besought the bishop to reconcile the penitent; should he assent, he examined the offender and imposed a fast of a fortnight, three, five, or seven weeks, at length giving absolution; after three episcopal admonitions a sinner was regarded as a heathen man and a publican. The *Council* of *Elvira* determined five years for accidental homicide, seven for murder or malice prepense; ten for adultery, or unchastity in priest.

In the seventh century public penance for secret sins was remitted; in the eighth, commuted for alms and prayers; in the tenth, in severe penance, a pilgrimage made by a man never passing two nights in one place, never eating meat, clipping hair or nails; if rich, he founded a church, built a bridge, made roads, or emancipated serfs; in the twelfth, generally for pilgrimages, and at length indulgences were given. In 1389, men in shirt and breeches, women in shifts, holding sacred images, stood during mass bareheaded and barefooted, and finally made an offering to the priest; in 1554 penitents stood wrapped in a white sheet, with a taper in one hand and a rod in the other during a sermon, after which they were struck on the head at Paul's Cross, and so reconciled. The two latest instances of such public penance in England occurred at *Bristol* in 1812, and at *Ditton, Cambs.,* 1849.*

"Dispelling with the Rod" was a public penance, performed on Good Friday, when the priest smote the hands of those who chose with a little bundle of rods. *Sir Thomas More* refers to it:

"Tindall is as lothe, good tender pernell, to take a little penaunce of the prieste, as the ladye was to come anye more to dyspelying that wepte ever for tender heart twoo dayes after when she talked of it, that the prieste had on good friday with the dyspelying rodde beaten her hard uppon her lylye white hands."

The old church accounts mention the purchase of these rods for Good Friday:

1510. *St. Mary-at-Hill, London.*

"For disseplynyng roddis, and nayles for the sepulchre, ij^d."

---

* In the primitive church penitents were placed in the "place of tears" near the great doors of the church, along with the catechumens, from Ash Wednesday till Maundy Thursday, where they begged those entering to pray for them.

The solemn ejection of penitents took place in England on Ash Wednesday, and is the "godly discipline" of solemn and public penance which the compilers of the Book of Common Prayer were of opinion, ought to be restored.* It was vigorously enforced by the Presbyterians during their short term of ascendancy in the seventeenth century, and is still in use in the ecclesiastical courts in the case of slander.

This reconciliation of the ejected penitents was accomplished in solemn procession to the west doors of the Cathedral, the bishop or priest in a red silk cope, accompanied by two deacons in albes and amices, preceded by an ash-coloured or sackcloth banner, but without a cross. At *Salisbury*, standing at the church door, the Penitentiary besought the bishop to reconcile the penitents ; at *Worcester* he distributed the ashes on the first day of Lent ; at *Rome* he preached on this day. At the great west porch door of *York Minster* sat Archbishop Sewal to exercise this office, and those who were obdurate were bound to the pillars and publicly whipped, whatever their degree. In parish churches the usage must have been very similar, for *Latimer* speaks of " poor Magdalene

---

* See *Rubric* at commencement of the Ash Wednesday Office.

under the board and in the belfry."* At *Vienna* the archbishop preached to the penitents at the west door of the cathedral, and at the end of the sermon, said three times, " Venite filii," the archdeacon adding " Accedite," whereupon all entered the church.†

At the mass on this day three large hosts only are consecrated, two to be reserved till the morrow,—one for the communion of the priest, and the other to be placed in the Sepulchre along with the cross. According to the *Sarum Use* the *Agnus* is not said, nor the *Pax* given, unless the bishop celebrates, when the *Gloria Patri* is sung at the Introit, and the *Gloria in Excelsis* is chanted, but not otherwise, and the Oilstock of the Holy Chrism is kissed in the place of the *Pax*.

After the Introit of this mass in both East and West the bishop, or a priest or ordinary minister acting for him on commission, consecrates the *Oleum, i.e.,* the *Chrism* or Holy Oil for use during the following year by a Solemn Office which signifies, says Cranmer, " principally the imperial and priestly dignity of Christ,

---

* Penitents of the worst class in early times stood without the church doors, begging of the prayers of those entering; even those let into the church had places separate and apart from other Christians.

† The Sermon on this day is still called *mandato* in Portugal.

and His being annointed with the spiritual unction of the Holy Ghost above all creatures, admonishing us of our state and condition; for as of chrism Christ is named, so of Christ we are called Christians; and it signifies defacing and abolishing of the rites and consecration of the Old Law, which were done in oil, and therefore at this time the old oil is burned and destroyed and new consecrated, signifying thereby our new regeneration in Christ and holy inunction which we have by His Holy Spirit."

This rite of consecrating Chrism is reserved to bishops only, by whom it is distributed to parish priests, but in early times oil was blessed for the anointing of the sick even by laymen. In the West, however, this office has been from an early period restricted to bishops, as by the *Council of Chalons* in the year 813, though it was not the practice in the early Gallican Church. In the East seven presbyters, or even one if necessity so require, can bless the oil for unction.

In the fifth century we find the ceremonial fixed to Maundy Thursday, and during the second of the three masses celebrated on that day, which in consequence was called the Mass of Chrism. However, in France, the *Council* of

Meaux, in 845, permitted the consecration on any day, as in primitive times ; and the Greeks, although regarding Maundy Thursday as the principal occasion, still follow the same practice, but reserve it to the patriarchs, who perform the office with great pomp.

The vase for keeping the chrism, was called from its shape, the chrism-paten.[1] In the tenth century it was fetched by a priest before Easter, or by a deacon or subdeacon, in thirteenth century. By the *Council of Melde*, three cruets were to be brought to the priest in which were the Baptismal Oil, Chrism and Oil for the sick. All that remained over from the last year being carefully consumed by fire.

Three kinds of oil are blessed by the bishop —i. *Oil of the Sick*, for the Sacrament of Extreme Unction ; ii. *Oil of Catechumens*, for anointing candidates prior to baptism ; iii. A mixture of oil and balsam called *Chrism*, which served for the anointing of altars, of the Sovereign at Coronations and for use at Baptism and Confirmation. After the blessing these oils were distributed to the parish priests of the diocese for use in their ministrations, the use of the oil for the confirmation of children being confined to the bishop, and that for the anointing of the Sovereign to the archbishop of

Ampulla.
ae time of
alarius it
covered
. a white
veil. See
alarius *de*
'es Officiis,
., cap. xii.
Sexta
etate cœna
aini.
pare the
ican *red*
ninisters,
white veil
hrisma-
. Also Mu-
ri, *Litur-*
Romana
s, Venetiis
3, t. ii.,
92. Feria v
1a Domini.

the province. In the Eastern Church, however, the priest is allowed to confirm with chrism.

By the *Auch Missal,* 1491, the *Gloria in Excelsis,* and *Credo* were only to be sung when Chrism was consecrated, and then only the deacon sings, "Ite Missa est," otherwise "Benedicamus Domino," and so mass ends in Evensong, when the Antiphon at Magnificat is doubled if chrism is consecrated.

After Evensong and refection which had immediately followed the Mass, the clergy proceeded to strip the altars and to wash the altar-stones, in signification of the stripping of Christ, or the flight of His Apostles, and in allusion to St. John xix. 34. It was customary also to do this at celebrations for the dead. (See *British Museum, Cottonian MSS., Domit,* No. 17.) The Strip=
ping and
Washing of
the Altars.

At this washing of the altars water was first blessed in the accustomed manner, without the Quire, and the altars beginning with the principal altar are washed with wine and water, privately blessed, by a priest, in an albe and red stole, attended by a deacon and subdeacon, cerofers and two boys carrying the wine and water, all in albes and amices. The first washing is with wine, then with water, the wine being poured upon the crosses of the altar-stone thus:

```
┌─────────────────────┐
│  2.            5.    │
│         1.           │
│  4.            3.    │
└─────────────────────┘
```

wine and water being afterwards spread over the whole slab and dried with a branch or brush of hard box, or some other trees such as blood-wort, or yew in memory of the crown of thorns. During the ceremony certain verses are sung. At *Chartres* and *Autun* the altar-slabs were rubbed with fragrant herbs on Good Friday, after the cleansing. The Churchwardens' Accounts of *St. Mary-at-Hill, London,* for the year 1503, have an entry for such a besom of box: "For box at the hallowing of the cherche to washe the auttyr, 1[d.]"

The *Liber Festivalis* thus refers to this ceremony:

"The altar stone betokeneth Christ's Body that was drawn on the cross as a skin of parchment on a harrow, so that all His bones might be told. And the besoms that the altar is washen with are the thorns that He was crowned with. The water and the wine that it is washen with betokeneth the blood and the water that ran down from His wound that was in His side pierced with a spear. The wine that is poured upon the altar on the five crosses betokeneth the blood that ran down from His principal wounds of His Body," etc.

The washing accomplished, the altars remain denuded until Holy Saturday, at the celebration, which desolation of the sacred places forcibly reminds us of the grief and mourning of the Church, and the abandonment in which our Saviour passed the night before and the day of His Passion.

The ceremony of washing the feet was to be performed in some convenient place. At *York Minster* the Maundy seats are probably those in the north quire aisle; at *Worcester* in the east alley of the cloisters is a bench table anciently used at the Maundy. On a stone bench in the east cloister at *Westminster* sat the twelve beggars whose feet the abbot washed with sundry solemn rites and signs of great humility. Under the nosing of the bench still remain the copper eyes from which hung the carpet on which he knelt during the performance of the ceremony. The rite was by no means confined to the Cathedrals and great monastic houses, but was performed by the Sovereign and other great and pious personages of the realm.*

The Washing Feet.

---

* In 1583, the French Ambassador (De Menainville) to Scotland washed the feet of thirteen poor men. The Pope washes the feet of thirteen priests at the *Lotio pedum.*

Neither was the ceremony altogether peculiar to Maundy Thursday. In some monasteries a Maundy occurred on every Saturday, the feet of as many poor people being washed in the eastern side of the cloisters as there were monks in the house. Some abbeys after the ceremony gave linen to the poor. Prior to the Norman Conquest there was a Maundy for washing the feet of three of the poor appertaining to a monastery, and distributing refection to them every day besides that of Maundy Thursday. *St. Oswald*, Archbishop of York, washed the feet of twelve poor-men and fed them every day.

The observance of this rite can be traced back to the *Pedilavium* (lavanda) of the fifth century, which followed the Holy Communion on Maundy Thursday. In the ancient church the feet of the newly baptized were washed on Easter Eve, in imitation of the washing of the disciples' feet by our Lord at His Maundy, and to which *St. Ambrose* alludes The *Pedilavium* was more recently observed at Holy Baptism at *Milan* and other places.*

---

* A similar ceremony exists among the Copts, where the priest on Ley'leb el-Gheeta's (Eve of the Festival of the Gheetas') after blessing water in the font, ties on a napkin as an apron, and, wetting the corner of a handkerchief with holy water, washes (wiping or touching with it) the feet of each member of the congregation. This ceremony is also performed on Maundy Thursday and the Festival of the Apostles (11th July).

At *Lichfield*, and probably in other cathedrals destitute of cloisters, the Maundy ceremony took place in quires; the stalls and aumbries on the north side of the quire at *York* having probably some connection with the ceremonial. At *Durham* the prior washed the feet of thirteen poor men in the cloister at 9 o'clock, and the monks the feet of children. The *Clugniacs* merely touched with wetted fingers the feet of three poor men; the *Benedictines* and *Cistercians* on the contrary scrupulously washed the feet of the brethren, the Abbot himself not being excused. In some places the poor whose feet were to be washed were present at mass, and were communicated with unconsecrated bread, probably from the Holy Loaf, without any formula of words. At the washing the officiant, girt with a linen towel, knelt bareheaded to wash, wipe, and afterwards kiss the right foot of those poor persons (generally thirteen in number to personify our Lord's Apostles) present for the ceremony, antiphons, etc., being sung meanwhile. After the ceremony gifts and a repast were given to them. At *Auch*, in 1555, a loaf and vegetables were given to each poor person whose feet had been washed. The *Ripon* Treasurer's Rolls contain payments for sugar, plate, comfits, etc., for the Maundy.

In *England* the ceremony of washing the feet was of old performed by the Sovereign in person as it still is in some countries abroad.

Edward II., in his nineteenth year, on the 21st March, washed the feet of fifty poor men.* On March 20th, 1361, an order was given to John de Newbury to buy and deliver to Thomas de Keynes, the King's Almoner, 200 ells of cloth of Candelwykstrete, 50 pairs of slippers, 2 short towels of Paris [cloth], and 4 ells of linen of Flanders, for next *Cena Domini.*†

Queen Elizabeth, at *Greenwich*, was wont to wash and kiss with the sign of the cross, the feet of as many poor persons as corresponded with her age.

James the Second is said to have been the last of our kings to perform this rite in person (in old chapel at Whitehall), and the prayers and ceremonies used by the House of Stuart are preserved in the Royal Cheque Book. According to this, after certain prayers and lessons, his Majesty, attended by the Lord Almoner and the White Staves, went to the poor men in order and sprinkled their feet with a sprig of hyssop dipped in water, and after wiping and kissing them, returned to his chair of state.

* Wardrobe Roll, 19, Ed. II., 25, 1 Q.R.
† Close Roll, 34, Ed. III.

Then followed certain anthems, during the singing of which the Lord Almoner distributed shoes and stockings, clothes, woollen and linen, purses, bread and fish; the whole being concluded with prayers having special reference to the act of washing and kissing the feet, and the Benediction. After the blessing the Lord Almoner called for wine and drank to all the poor the King's health, bidding them be thankful to God, and pray for the King.

Upon the cessation of the ceremony by the Hanoverian Sovereigns it was deputed to the Lords Almoners, the Archbishop of York, who performed it in the palace of Whitehall till the year 1731. On Thursday, April 23rd, 1736, the Rev. Dr. Gilbert, Sub-Almoner, in the absence of the Archbishop of York, distributed at Whitehall, to 53 poor men and women, his Majesty's alms, viz.: to each, three ells of Holland, a piece of cloth for a coat, a pair of shoes and stockings, a purse with 20 shillings, and 53 silver pence, a loaf of bread, and a wooden platter of fish. In Duke Street Chapel, his grace the Archbishop of York, assisted by Drs. Gilbert and Hatter, washed the feet of so many poor persons. In the year following, his Majesty's alms were distributed to 54 poor men and women, but the washing ceremony was omitted. Since which time it has been disused, though several minor parts of the office are still retained; the only symbolical act remaining being the girding of the Almoner and his attendants with long linen cloths, which they retain as their perquisite. According to ancient usage, the yeomen of the guard, who line the chapel on the occasion, were always covered until within the last fifteen years.

Archbishop Cranmer, writing of this ceremony, says: "Our Lord did wash the feet of His desciples, teaching humbleness and very love and charity by His example. It is a laudable custom to wash the altars and to prepare with all cleanness the places where the most blessed Sacrament shall be ministered; and also to be for us a remembrance that as those things inanimate are washed and cleansed for that purpose, so we ought much more to prepare and wash our minds and consciences at all times, and especially at this time for the more worthy receiving of the same most high Sacrament. We, in like manner, as Christ washed His desciples' feet at His Maundy, should be ready at all times to do good unto our Christian brothers, yea, even to wash their feet, which seemeth to be the most humble and lowly act that we can do unto them."

After the ceremony of the washing of the altar and of the Maundy at *Sarum Cathedral,* and probably other places, all adjourned to the Chapter House, where the " Potum Caritatis " or " Loving Cup " was blessed and dispensed to each by way of refreshment after their labours. There was no special service for this, a special gospel (St. John xiii., 16-38; xiv., 1-31) only being read during the partaking of the cup by the clergy. At monastic, and domestic, refection, on this night, at *Durham,* a wooden bowl or mazer, called the *Judas Cup,* was used. The ceremony was probably a remnant of the old Agapæ; the *Third Council of Carthage* permitted a supper after Holy Communion on this day. In both East and West the monks supped together after the Maundy.

The Adoration of "Creeping to" the Holy Cross.

FROM the earliest times the Church has ever commemorated with especial veneration the most prominent events in the life of her Master and Lord—His Birth, Death, Resurrection and Ascension each receiving due celebration. As time went on into the earlier Middle Ages, when Faith was growing dim and worldliness seemed almost to have got the master hand, the Church, in order to keep the great facts of Christian mystery continually before the minds of her children, instituted special rites and ceremonies to that end. Thus at Christmas the spectacle of the Divine Birth was pourtrayed, and in the Passion-tyde the " Blessed Burying" and Resurrection.

On Good Friday, after None, the ceremony known as the *Adoration* of the Cross, more familiarly called the " Creeping to the Cross," took place. At the words, in the solemn reading of the *Passion* (according to *St. John* vv. i.-xix. v. 37), "They parted my raiment among them," two ministers in surplices[1] removed two linen cloths from off the altar, which had been placed there for that purpose, and after the Collects for all mankind, two other priests, in albes without apparels, and feet unshod, held up between them the veiled cross behind the high altar, towards the right side, while the "*Improperia*" or reproaches (an expansion of Malachi iii. 3, 4), were sung. The priests then uncovered the cross—(for when Christ gave up the *G*host the Temple Veil was rent in twain, and from that time all the Mosaic Law was manifested to the *G*entiles)—by the right side of the altar, and the Antiphon "Behold the holy cross," etc., being sung, the cross is solemnly set down upon a cushion on the third step from the altar :

> 1550. July 14th, 4 Edward VI. *London, St. Dunstan in the East.*
>
> "*Item*, iij Cosshyns of Red* sylke and golde for good frydaye for the Crosse."†

In the Inventory of Westminster Abbey, taken at the Dissolution, appears "a crosse for

[1] "*Non medis pedibus*" is the rubrical direction at Albi, but bare feet appears to have been the general rule.

---

* Red would appear to have been the colour for Good Friday. 1550. (4 Ed. VI.) *St. Dunstan in the East, London.* "*Item*, a vestment of Red for good ffrydaye with stole and ffannell."

† P. R. Office. Ch. Gds. Exch. Q.R. ₅⁴/₈₄.

good Friday," but it would appear that the altar cross was generally requisitioned for the ceremony, as it was for processions.

The cross thus deposited, two priests seat themselves near it, one on the right side, the other on the left, and the veneration commences, the hymns " *Pange lingua* " and " *Vexilla regis prodeunt* " being sung meanwhile. After the adoration by the clerks, etc. (at *Sarum Cathedral*), the cross was carried through the midst of the Quire, attended by the candle-bearers, and set down before some altar, where it was venerated by the people, who saluted it with a kiss, genuflecting as they approached at every three paces. At its approach they bowed as low as possible, and then with extended arms took it and kissed it. (*Aug. Sacr.* II., 316.)

According to Dom Claude de Vert (*Explication simple litterale et historique des ceremonies de L'Eglise,* written towards the close of the seventeenth century, and which gives a complete exposition of the custom), it began at Jerusalem in the fourth century, *i.e.,* after the time that St. Helen, the mother of Constantine, had discovered the cross, of which he says : she left a part to be preserved by the Bishop of Jerusalem, and sent the rest to the Emperor, her son. Every year on *Good* Friday the

Bishop of Jerusalem exposed this part of the true cross to be adored: that is, saluted and reverenced by all the people. Henceforth this ceremony of the exposition and adoration of the cross was communicated abroad to churches, which possessed some trifling morsel or small portion of the same sacred wood, of which St. Cyril of Jerusalem (Catech., 4-10) reports great numbers as existing in the middle of the fourth century, and then by extension and imitation among the rest of the churches in the world; where in default of some part of the true cross, common crosses were substituted, representing that of our Lord which were exposed to the worship of the faithful; yet retaining always these words, *Ecce lignum crucis, in quo salus mundi perpendit.*

This alleged discovery of the very cross on which our Saviour Christ suffered is said to have taken place about A.D. 326. *Eusebius* (d. 338) is silent on the subject of the discovery, but *St. Cyril* of *Jerusalem*, who delivered his Catechetical Lectures about 347, speaks of the Holy Cross as discovered. (See *Baronii Annales,* sub anno 326.) *St. Ambrose* (395), and *St. Chrysostom*, about 394, speak of three crosses as discovered. By the close of the fourth century there was a general belief in the discovery. The *Inventio Crucis* in the calendar prefixed to the Book of Common Prayer on the 3rd of May, on which feast (but not on that of the Exaltation) the cross was worshipped in a somewhat similar manner as upon Good Friday, when it was kissed with great reverence. In the East the Third Sunday in Lent (Occuli) is called the Adoration of the Cross, while in the Greek Church the cross is very similarly adored on the Feast of its Exaltation.

The earliest allusion to the right of adoration, as a stated ceremony is perhaps in the *Ordo Romanus,* said to be compiled or composed by Gelasius, but subtracted from, added to, and revised by Gregory the Great, c. 597. In this is the *Ordo in die Parasceves, ubi mos est salutiferam salutare crucem.* This *Ordo* ordains that at even the cross is prepared before the altar, a space intervening between it and the altar, carried by two acolytes. Then after certain texts of Scripture followed the anthem,—*Ecce lignum crucis, in quo salus mundi perpendit: venite adoremus.* Then comes the Pope alone, and adoring kisses the cross. Then the bishops, priests, deacons, and others in order, last of all the people. After sundry genuflections and prayers, follows the ancient hymn of the Latin Church, concluding thus:

" Crux fidelis inter omnes
Arbor una nobilis," etc.

This hymn concluded, and the cross saluted, it was deposited in its place. Such in substance was the ancient rite of the Roman Church.

St. Isidore of *Seville* does not appear to allude to this ceremony, but *Albinus Flaccus Alcuinus* (Pseudo-Alcuin) (d. 804) alludes to the salutation of the cross, more at length in his exposition of the *Ordo Romanus*, adding that sometimes it was laid on a cushion in a side chapel. *Amalarius*, Archbishop of Treves, in the early part of the ninth century—(he died 837), treats of " *De adoratione sancta crucis*," in his work " *De ecclesiasticis officiis*," *i.e.*, that the cross should be prepared before the altar, and saluted by all with a kiss. *Rabanus Maurus* (d. 856) alludes also to the rite when treating of " *De Parasceve*," and so *Durandus* in the well-known *Rationale divinorum officiorum* of the thirteenth century, but his comments are full of allegorical and mystical meanings.

The *Canons* of *Archbishop Ælfric* (957) required the faithful to pay their adoration, and to greet the cross with a kiss. " Let all of them on Good Friday greet the rood of God with kissing." (*Aug. Sacr.* II., 316). " Let all priests admonish their parishioners," says

Bishop Henry of Sisteron (1240-50), "to teach their children from the age of seven and upwards the Paternoster and the Credo, and on Good Friday bring them with them to the church to kiss the cross, and on Easter Day to receive the body of Christ, having, however, previously confessed." The Constitution of *Giles* of *Bridport*, Bishop of Sarum, 1256, is to the same purpose: "Let no one presume on Easter Day to approach the Body of Christ unless he has first confessed and adored the cross." (Wilkins, i. 704). In the notes to the "*Northumberland House Book*" we read that the ushers were to lay "a carpet for the Kinge to creepe to the crosse upon"; the Queen and her ladies were also to "creepe to the crosse."

Langland in his *Vision* of *Piers Plowman* (1362-1400) tells how at the end of Piers' eighth dream, the bells rang to the Resurrection, and awakening, he calls to his wife and daughter, saying, "Arise, and go to reverence *God's* Resurrection, and creep on knees to the cross" and to mass and sacrament.

In the articles about religion set out by the Convocation, and published by the King's (Henry VIII.) authority, 1536, one is of *Rites and Ceremonies*, viz. :—"As concerning the rites and ceremonies of Christ's Church—

creeping to the crosse, and humbling ourselves
to Christ on Good Friday, and offering there-
unto Christ before the same, and kissing of it
in memory of our redemption by Christ made
upon the cross; setting up the sepulchre of
Christ, whose body after his death was buried;
. . . . -and all other like laudable customs,
rites and ceremonies be not to be contemned
and cast away, but to be used and continued as
things good and laudable; to put us in remembrance of those spiritual things that they do
signify, not suffering them to be forgotten, or
to be put in oblivion, but renewing them in the
memories from time to time; but none of these
ceremonies have power to remit sin, but only to
stir and lift up our minds unto God by whom
only our sins be forgiven." This was confirmed
by the Rationale or explanation of ceremonies
drawn up about 1541-3. (See Collier, vol. v.,
pp. 106-24.)

The *Beehiue of the Romish Churche*, a satirical
production, translated out of Dutch into English by *George Gilpin* the elder, and newly
imprinted in 1580, adverts to the custom thus
"And besides she (the Church of Rome) had
more ordered and charged that we should upon
the *Good* Friday after Maundy Thursday,
devoutly and sadly creeping along the ground

upon our bare knees, worship the cross, and there bestow a good fat offering and liberal almes to the benefit and maintenance of the poore Priests."

The author of the *Durham Rites* says that at that place about the time of Wolsey, the " Cross was laid upon a velvet cushion, having St. Cuthbert's arms upon it all embroider'd with gold," set upon the "lowest greeses or steps in the quire," where two monks held the picture [image]* of our Saviour betwixt them, sitting on either side of it. And then " one of the said monks did rise, and went a pretty space from it, and setting himself upon his knees with his shoes put off, very reverently he crept upon his knees unto the said cross, and most reverently did kiss it; and after him the other monk did so likewise, and then they sate down on either side of the said cross, holding it betwixt them. Afterward the prior came forth of his stall, and did sit him down upon his knees with his shoes off in like sort, and did creep also unto the said cross, and all the monks after him, one after another, in the same manner and order; in the meantime the whole quire singing a hymn."

---

* " Picture " and " image " were at the period synonymous terms.

Chambers, in his *Book of Days* (i. 418), says a dressed-up figure of Christ, mounted on a crucifix, was borne around the altar by two priests, with doleful chants; then laying it on the ground with great tendernesse they fell beside it, kissed its hands and feet with piteous sighs and tears, the other priests doing the like in succession. After came the people to worship, each bringing some little gift, such as corn and eggs

From this it would appear to have been customary to make offerings at this " creeping to the cross." The Wardrobe Accounts for 1252-3 and 1264-5 show an entry of such an oblation of five shillings made by Henry III., " in adoration of the Holy Cross." Edward II. too " adores the Cross " but on the morning of Easter, and other Sovereigns continue to adore it at Easter, probably when taken out of the Easter Sepulchre. The offerings thus bestowed were both in money and kind, when in the former they were known as " *Creeping Silver.*"*

Moreover the Household Books of Henry IV. and Edward IV. tell us that the metal out of which the *cramp rings*, anciently blessed and

---

* The Sepulchre at *East Kirby, Lincolnshire*, has partly projecting from the ledge, a stone basin, without perforation, intended, no doubt, to receive these oblations.

distributed on Good Friday, were made, was the King's offering to the crosse upon that day. The following entry occurs in 7 and 8, Henry IV. (1406) :

> " In oblacionibus Domini Regis factis adorando crucem in cappella infra manerium suum de Eltham, die Parasceive, in precis trium nobilium auri et v solidorum sterlynge xxv^{s.}"

The king "coming in state into his chapel, he found a crucifix laid upon a cushion and a carpet spread on the ground before it. The monarch crept along the carpet to the crucifix, as a token of his humility, and there blessed the cramp rings in a silver basin, kneeling all the time, with his almoner likewise kneeling by his side. After this was done, the queen and her ladies came in, and likewise crept to the cross." These cramp rings were thought to derive their efficacy from the ring of St. Edward the Confessor, kept at Westminster.*

Such entries as the following are met with in the old parish accounts :

> 1514. *Bristol. St. Ewen* (destroyed).
> " *Item*, yn Offeryng money to the Crose."

---

* For further particulars concerning them see Chambers' *Book of Days.*

1541. London. *St. Margaret, Westminster.*
"Received on Good Friday, for crepinge
to the Cross the same yere, v^{d.}"

Each worshipper would bring some little
gift, if not money then in kind, corn, eggs,
apples, etc. John Bale (Declaration of Bonner's Articles, 1554) censures "To holde forth
the Crosse for Egges on Good Friday."
William Kethe, in a Sermon preached on
January 17th, 1570, at Blandford Forum,
Dorset, speaks of offering unto Christ Eggs
and Bacon to be in hys favour till Easter Day
was passed. Also Herbert in his "*Short Description of Antichrist*" (published 1579), notes
the custom of "creepinge to the Cross with
eggs and apples." These things being devoted
with the alms to the sustenance of poor clergy.

This creeping to and salutation of Christ's
Holy Cross lingered on into the early years of
Elizabeth, when, with other kindred rites, it fell
into disuse. In the last year but one (May 6th,
1546) of Henry VIII., we find Mr. Devorouxe,
Lord Ferrar's son, being examined before the
Privy Council touching words spoken by him in
matters of religion, as of creeping to the cross,
holy water, etc. (Proc. of Privy Council, fol.
193). In the Royal Injunctions issued in the
following year (1. Edward VI.) no allusion is

made to the ceremonies of Good Friday or Easter Day, but in a royal proclamation set forth on the 6th February of the next (his second) year, against those who do innovate, alter, and heave down any rite or ceremony, in the Church of their private authority, it was provided that for not creeping to the cross, no man hereafter be imprisoned or otherwise punished, which would show the observance of the custom was left a matter of indifference, to be observed or not at the individual will.

In the *Visitation Articles* of *Cranmer* of this same second year, the question is put to the clergy whether they had upon *Good Friday* last past the sepulchres with their lights, having the sacrament therein; and in certain further *Articles,* without date to be followed and observed according to the King's Majesty's injunctions and proceedings, the *ninth* enjoins amongst other rites, that no man maintain sepulchres, or creeping to the cross.

Yet for all this the old usages still found great favour, as the third Sermon of Latimer before Edward VI., in the Lent of 1549, shows

"As ther was a doctor that preached, the kinges maiesty hath his holy water, he crepeth to the crosse, and then thei have nothynge but the Kynge! the kinge l in

their mouthes. These be my good
people that muste have their mouthes
stopte," etc.

In Scotland the custom was observed at Dunbar
as late as 1568, by the congregation barelegged
and barefooted.

Upon the accession of Mary an endeavour
was made to bring about a revival of many disused customs as shown by a letter with articles
sent by that Queen to Bishop of London in
March, 1553-4. The thirteenth is "that the
laudable and honest ceremonies which were
wont to be used, frequented and observed in the
church, be also hereafter frequented, used, and
observed." Similar injunctions were issued by
Cardinal Pole, in the diocese of Gloucester,
in which one appears touching the laity, "that
all parishioners shall obediently use all the
godly ceremonies of the church as (amongst
others therein enumerated) creeping to the
cross."

Sometimes for this ceremony a special cross
was used, though generally, as aforesaid, the
altar cross seems to have been brought into
requisition. At the Cathedral of Durham there
was an image of our Lady, called of Bolton,
standing over the second altar in the south
aisle, which was made to open with gimmers

(hinges—two leaves?) from the breast downwards, and within was painted the image of the Saviour, finely gilt, holding up His hands; and betwixt His hands a fair and large crucifix, all of gold, which crucifix was to be taken out every Good Friday, and every man (another MS. says monk) crept unto it that was then in the church, after which it was hung up again within the said image. (*Rites of Durham,* p. 26.)

After its adoration the cross was reverently carried back to the high altar, and after mass was to be washed with wine and water, and the ablutions given to the priests and people to drink after the Good Friday communion in memory of the blood and water which flowed from the side of the crucified Saviour.* After this ceremonial washing the cross was to be carried to the sepulchre, thence to be triumphantly carried on Easter Day in the morning. On Good Friday, after the adoration of the Cross, says *Beleth,* the reserved Host was set on the altar, and after Communion, Vespers were sung.

---

* According to the *Sarum Missal,* "Adoratio crucis in Parasceve" (p. 329) one cross may be exposed till shortly before Evensong. Another authority states a silver cross was used on Good Friday.

The Burial of the Cross and Host in the Easter Sepulchre.*

AT first it was the cross only after its adoration on Good Friday that -was buried in the Sepulchre, the reserved Host only being buried with it in process of time. The exact date when this took place is uncertain, but the thirteenth century is thought to be somewhat about the period when the devotion of the faithful came naturally to be directed to the Host rather than to the cross which still continued to be buried with it.

The origin of the sepulchre rite is equally uncertain—some inclining to the suggestion that its source lay in the old Mystery Plays which were of old performed in the churches, and indeed some of the characteristics of the

* A small portion of this paper appeared in the "Nineteenth Century" for May, 1895.

K

Sepulchre Offices themselves would lend much support to such a theory; while others think the ceremony arose as occasion or devotion required, as did the Christmas Crib and other like devotions.

In some of the early monasteries and cathedrals the Cross after its adoration on Good Friday, was washed with wine and water and wiped with a towel at the door of the sepulchre, the quire singing in an under-tone the Responsories, *Tenebræ factæ sunt*, etc., etc., which done, the ablution was given to the priests and people to drink after this day's communion, in memory of the blood and water which flowed from the side of the crucified Saviour. *John of Avranches* mentions this washing of the Cross as occurring just before the completion of the Adoration, and also of the drinking of the wine and water after the Communion. After this washing the cross was wrapped or swathed in linen or silk cloths, and carried to the place of its deposition, either in a space within the back of the altar—under the altar stone—or in the portable or permanent tomb known as the Easter Sepulchre, across which a curtain or veil was drawn until Easter morning.[1] At *Tours*, the Canons, on Good Friday, recited the Hours, not in their stalls,

6, *St. ten, Cole- Street, yll coffyn e crosse.*'

but standing round a tomb of marble.*   In the *Exeter Ordinale* (fo. 45), the direction for Good Friday and Easter Eve is very similar: " Let Evensong also be said at the close of office, privately, before the Sepulchre of our Lord, all being gathered in front of the high altar."

It would appear that minor altars themselves were occasionally hollowed out as Easter Sepul chres (*v.* Wilkins, *Concilia,* i. 497), and *Martene* tells us that the Host was to be deposited on Good Friday *in una ¡parte altaris,* and the *Roman rubric* directs: *Hodie paretur locus aptus in aliqua capella ecclesiæ, vel altari.*   The altar in the rood loft may have been used in some places as the " Sepulchre awlter " of *St. Lawrence, Reading,* in "ye loft over the chan- cell crosses, where the* sepulchre lighte dyd stand."†   In the inventory of *Lee, Kent* (6 Edward VI.), mention is made of " a grete stone before thighe altar," which may

---

* This is one of the earliest references to an Easter Sepulchre. No mention of a sepulchre is made in any of the Synodical or Provincial Constitutions relating to church furniture as essential to a church, in *Wilkins' Concilia.* The earliest account of a sepulchre thus set up, yet met with, occurs in an inventory of 1214.

† Kerry. *Account of the Sepulchre Altar, St. Lawrence, Reading,* anno 1498.

have been used as a filling for the space when not in use, *e.g. :*

> 1480-2. *London. St. Andrew Hubbard, East Cheap.*
>
> "*Item,* paid to a man for taking oute of a Stone, and setting in of the bace of the Resurreccion, that the tabernacle stondeth vpon, iiij^{d.}"
>
> "*Item,* paid to a carver for making bace and for lyne for tabernacle cloth, xxij^{d.}"

In *Cistercian Churches,* and at *Pisa, Bourges, Chartres,* and *Rheims,* the middle or mattin altar was used for the reservation of the veiled cross on Good Friday, which was borne in procession by two clerics singing the anthem, "*Popule Meus.*"

In progress of time a fuller ceremonial came into vogue, much of which is comparatively modern. Some of the monasteries and even cathedrals which have saved their rites as they were in the sixteenth century have only a very small portion of the ceremony.

The precise date of the burial of the Blessed Sacrament with the cross cannot be easily determined, but a thirteenth century French MS. shows that the ceremonial described in St. Dunstan's *Regularis Concordia* was at that period transferred to the Blessed Sacrament,* which the *Sarum Directorium*† of the same date confirms, as it mentions the taking of the Body of our Lord from the Sepulchre on Easter morning, as well as of the Cross. Yet for all this at *Hereford*, prior to the fifteenth century, although the Missal orders one of the Hosts consecrated on Good Friday to be placed with the Cross in the Sepulchre, the Cross *only* was so buried; and the *York Missal*, though giving directions about the burial of the Cross in the Sepulchre, does not explicitly order the Blessed Sacrament to be placed with it.‡

Again we find in a certain Norman treatise on the Church Offices, dated 1079, by the Archbishop of Rouen (John, brother of Duke Richard of Normandy) a contemporary of Lanfranc, mentions both usages—the burial of the Cross and Host,—and gives directions for the honourable reservation of the Blessed Sacrament from Thursday to Friday, ordering a light to be kept burning before It until the extinction of the last taper in the "Tenebræ" Office on the Thursday night. §

---

* *Office du Sépulcre selon l'usage de l'Abbaye d'Origny*, Paris, 1858.

† Edited by Dr. Rock, vol. iv., p. 53.

‡ The *Arbuthnot Missal* directs both Host and Cross to be placed in the Sepulchre. A chalice with wine, as well as the Corpus Domini, were buried at *Albi*, Aquitaine.

§ See Migne, *Patrologia*, tom. cxlvii. p. 50.

The ceremony of the burial of the Host with the Cross in the Easter or Holy Sepulchre was nothing less than an imitation of the burial rites usual in the Middle Ages, which is abundantly proved by the Inventories and Parish Accounts where the use of bier, palls, high stone tombs, lights, watchers are found—in fact all the pomp and ceremony of the mediæval burial of a person of high degree. Thus we find Becon, the chaplain of Archbishop Cranmer, discoursing in his " *Acts of Christ and Antichrist* " (1564) as follows :

> " Christ was buried in a poor monument, sepulchre, or grave, without any funeral pomp." " Antichrist is buried in a glorious tomb, well gilt and very gorgeously set out with many torches, and with great solemnity, and with angels gloriously portured that bear his soul to heaven."

And the Author of the *Beehive of the Romish Churche* :

> " They make the grave in a high place in the churche, where men must go up many steps, whiche are decked with blacke cloth from aboue to beneath, and up on every step standeth a silver candlestick with a waxe candle burning

in it, and there doe walk souldiers in harnesse as bright as St. George, which keep the frame, tyll the priestes come and take hem up, and then commeth sodenly a flashe of fire, wherewith they are all afraide and fal downe, and then up starts the man,* and they begin to sing Alleluia on al hands, and the clocke striketh 11."

The author of the *Rites of Durham* (written about 1593), probably an eye witness of what he describes, pictures for us the ceremony about the time of Cardinal Wolsey:

" Within the Abbey Church of Durham on Good Friday there was a marvellous solemn service, in which service time, after the Passion sung, two of the oldest monks took a goodly large crucifix, all of gold, of the picture of our Saviour Christ nayled upon the Cross. [*Here follows a description of the Adoration of the Cross.*] The service being ended, the said two monks carried the Cross to the Sepulchre with great reverence [*i.e.*, and with lights, and incense, and singing], (which Sepulchre was set up in the morning on the north side of the

---

* The Crucifix is taken from the tomb.

Quire, nigh unto the High Altar, before
the service time), and there did lay it
within the said Sepulchre with great
devotion, with another picture [image]
of our Saviour in whose Breast they did
enclose with great reverence the Most
Holy and Blessed Sacrament of the
Altar, censing and praying unto It
upon their knees a great space, and
setting two tapers lighted before It,
which did burn till Easter Day in the
morning, at which time It was taken
forth."

Thomas Naogeorgus, in his *Regnum Papisti-
cum*, published in Latin verse at Basil, in 1559,
and "Englyshed," or rendered into English
verse by Barnabe Googe, in 1570, brings the
whole scene vividly before us :

" *Good Friday.*

Two Priestes the next day following upon their shoulders beare,
The image of the Crucifix, about the Altar nere :
Another Image doe they get, like one but newly deade,
With legges stretcht out at length and hands, upon his body spreade :
And him with pompe and sacred song, they bear unto his grave,
His body all being wrapt in lawne and silkes and sarcenet brave,

   .   .   .   .

And least in grave he should remaine without some companie,
The singing bread is laid with him, for more idolatrie :
The Priest the Image worships first, as fallest to his turne,
And frankensence and sweete perfumes, before the bread doth burne ;

With tapers all the people come, and at the barriers stay,
Where down upon their knees they fall, and night and day they pray :
And violets and every kinde of flowres about the grave
They straw, and bring in all their giftes, and presents that they have."[*]

It would appear that in some instances a special cross was used for the ceremony as at *Durham*, and as the following ·

> 1470. (10 Edward IV.) *St. Margaret Pattens, London.*
>
> " *Item*, a nod[r] crosse for the sepulcur havyng relikes therein."

The Easter Sepulchres may be divided into five classes :

> (i.) A simple walled recess, as at *Bottesford, Lincoln.*
>
> (ii.) A tomb under which a founder or builder either of the church or sepulchre, by special privilege was buried, as at *Hurstmonceaux, Sussex.*
>
> (iii.) A temporary structure sumptuously decorated, as at *St. Mary Redcliffe, Bristol.*
>
> (iv.) A vaulted enclosure richly carved, as at *Lincoln Cathedral.*
>
> (v.) A chapel, as at *Winchester.*

---

[*] Another similar account says that boys with clappers went before singing, and the Sexton bore a light presumably before the Holy Sacrament, the people kneeling down, kissing the ground, holding up hands and beating their breasts.

The first class—the simple arched recess more or less ornamented—is the earliest form of the permanent Easter Sepulchre, and none date earlier than the thirteenth century. They are generally to be found in the smaller or village churches in the north chancel wall (but not always, as witness the example in *Broken-hurst Church, Hants,* which is on the south side), adjacent to the High Altar, and it is very probable that many of the recesses called aumbries were used for this purpose, as they were for the reserved Host, altar and other sacramental vessels and vestments. Fine examples of such a recess is the double one in *Bottesford Church, Lincoln ;* at *Stanton St. John, Oxford; Hempstead cum Eccles, Norfolk ; Gar-thorpe, Leicestershire ; St. Martin's, Canterbury,* and *Cubbington* and *Long Itchington, Warwick-shire,* the latter canopied and probably of thirteenth century date.

The second class are those tombs of founders either of Church or Sepulchre, so frequently found placed against the north chancel wall of churches, upon which as within the simple arched recess were placed the carved and painted erections of wood which have been placed in the third class. A well-authenticated instance is the tomb of *Thomas Windsor,*

Esquire, dated 1485, in *Stanwell Church, Middlesex*, which by the testimony of his will, dated 1479 and proved in 1485, was built for this purpose. 'I will,' he says, 'that there be made a playn tombe of marble of a competent height, to the entent that yt may ber the blessid body of our Lord and the sepulture, at the tyme of Eastre, to stond upon the same; and myne Ames and a Scriptur convenient to be set about the same tombe.' This tomb has been removed to the west end of the north aisle, and the brasses (effigies of the deceased and wife which were placed upright in the wall) have disappeared.* *Eleanore*, second wife and widow of Sir Roger Townsend, a Justice of the Common Pleas in the time of Henry VIII., dying in 1500, by her will dated November 9, 1499, desired her body to be buried by the High Altar in the north-east part of the chancel of the church of *Rainham St. Mary*, and a new tomb to be made for her husband's and her bones; upon which tomb was to be cunningly graven a Sepulchre for Easter Day, if a chapel be not made at her decease, in which case the tomb was to be made there, and both her husband's and her bones buried therein. The

* See Collins's *Peerage*, vol. iv., p. 74, ed. 1779, and *Testamenta Vetusta*, p. 352.

chapel was not erected, and a tomb stands in the chancel, but without any inscription.*

In 1531, *Thomas, Lord Dacre*, in his will writes: 'My body to be buried in the parish church of *Hurst Monceaux*, on the north side of the High Altar. I will that a tomb be there made for placing the Sepulchre of our Lord, with all fitting furniture thereto, in honour of the Most Blessed Sacrament.' Three years afterwards this tomb was erected of Caen stone and Petworth marble, and rises with its canopy of niches and tracery nearly the whole height of the church.† *Sir H. Colet*, father of the Dean, lies at Stepney, 'at Sepulchre.'

Similar tombs are at *West Dean, Sussex, Alfriston* and *Stoke Charity, Hants*, and *Stanton Harcourt, Oxon*. The altar tomb of *Christopher Urswych*, 1521, which was against the north chancel wall of *Hackney* old church, was probably used for the same purpose, and to which an allusion may be intended in the words of the black letter inscription · '*hic sepultus carnis resurreccionem in aduentu christi expectat.*' At Ardley, Oxford, the final of the Easter Sepulchre has the words 'Non Est.' *St. Matt.* xxviii. 6.

---

* Blomefield's *Norfolk*, vii. p. 132.
† *Testamenta Vetusta*, p. 653.

Upon these often richly sculptured altar tombs, as also within the less elaborate and more simple arched recesses, the movable sepulchre of wood, richly carved, gilded, and painted with sacred Passion Story and legend, were set and surrounded by a frame which served a double purpose of keeping off the crowds of devotees as well as a support for the numerous lights by which it was illuminated.*

As every village church had its Easter Sepulchre these portable wooden sepulchres must have been very numerous. They took the shape of a gabled coffer or coped chest or closet of wood, very similar, if not identical with the portable shrine for relics, carried about in procession, or the mortuary chests which rest upon the choir screen at Winchester.† The sepulchre, when not set within the recess or upon the altar tomb, stood upon a frame fashioned as a bier—in fact it was a diminutive coped coffin upon its bier, a fact proved by many inventories and particularly by one taken at the time of the Reformation at *Stallingbrock, Lincolnshire,* where the sepulchre

---

* In 1558, the old sepulchre and 'the toumbe of brycke' of *St. Mary's, Reading,* was sold. Coat's *Hist. Reading,* p. 130.

† 1536. *London. St. Christopher-le-Stock.* "A sepulcre of silver for relics" (sold); another of "silver and overgilt with the flesh of St. Christopher."

was positively used " as a bear [bier] to carie the dead corps " to burial—the whole arrangement being very similar to those of the modern Egyptians for conveying to the grave the corpses of females and boys.[1] The following sketch represents the Egyptian bier with its pall.

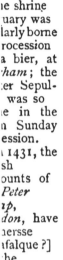

The Churchwardens' Accounts and Parish Inventories, especially those taken at the Reformation period, bear superabundant witness to the number and construction of these portable sepulchres, as also of their erection when required for use; and destruction, by burning and breaking, in the early years of Queen Elizabeth, over fifty being destroyed out of as many as 153 Lincolnshire churches.

A few examples must suffice :

1455. *St. Ewen, Bristol.*

" The apparail of tre (wood) and Ire (iron) made for the sepulcre with the clothes steyned ther to ordeyned."

ıe shrine uary was larly borne rocession a bier, at *ham*; the :er Sepul- was so ıe in the ı Sunday ession.
ı 1431, the sh ounts of *Peter ıp, don,* have ıersse ıfalque ?] :he lcre," and 540 (27 . VIII.) *low. Item,* l unto :et for dynge of ıre for the lcre, ijd."

5. Hen. VI *London. St. Mary Hill.*
 " For the Sepulchre, for divers nayles and wyres and glue, 9$^{d.}$ ob."

1480-2. *London. St. Andrew Hubbard, East Cheap.*
 " *Item*, for a Coffyn to laye in the Crossis and mendyng the ff'rame, vj^{d} "

1540. (27 Hen. VIII.) *Ludlow.*
 " *Item*, paid to Thomas Hunt for mendynge of the crofer for y^{e} sepulcre, ij^{d}."
 " *Item*, payd for borde nayle and lathe neale for the same cofer, ij^{d}."

1552. *Kent (St. Elphege), Canterbury.*
 " *Item*, a sepulcre with a frame whereof the parson hath the one side."

Surrey. Wandsworth.
 " Receivede of John Edwyn for broken tymber and waynescote and the sepulchr by the consent of the parish."

1554. *London. St. Michael's, Cornhill.*
 " *Item*, paide for makynge of frame of the Sepulker."
 " Paide for hookes & staples to the same frame."

1555. *Ludlow.*
 " Paid to John Blunt for the tymber of the sepulcre, and his help to makynge of the same, vj$^{s.}$ "

"Paid to Stephen Knight, for makynge of viij rynges and viij staples and a hoke of yron for the sepulcre, xii^{d.}"

1559. "Payd for a clasp of iron to set upon the frame of the sepulcre."

1555. *London. St. Michael's, Cornhill.*

"Paide for the Joyenour for makinge the sepullere, the Paskall and the Tenebras to the same," and for "nailes and tacks" for the sepulchre—a frequent charge in these accounts.

At *St. Mary, Woolnorth,* "a sepulchre chest that stood in the quere," cost xx^{d.}; mention being also made of "a sharyne [shrine?] for the sepulture covered with a clothe of tyssue."

That they were erected especially for the sepulchre ceremony and taken down afterwards is equally proved by these same accounts :

1513. *St. Lawrence, Reading.*

"*Item,* payd for settying upp the frame aboute the sepulcre;" in 1514, five pence was paid for ale to the carpenters at the removal of the sepulchre.

1516. *St. Mary Hill, London.*

"In part for a chest to lay the sepulchre in."

1520. *St. Margaret, Westminster.*

"For setting up of *God's house* and taking it down again."

1552. *Thame, Oxon.*

"*Item,* for makyng . . ye sepulcre, iij^{d.}" . . . "for naile in settinge upe the sepulcrye, j^{d.}"

1557. *Ludlow.*

"*Item,* to him for iij dayes worke in settynge up the sepulcre, xvij^{d.}"

That these sepulchre chests were often of value and of much artistic merit is evidenced by the new sepulchre at *St. Lawrence's, Reading,* costing the considerable sum for those days of £4 13s. 10d.,* when ten years later (1521), that at *St. Andrew Hubbard, East Cheap,* was obtained at the low figure of 8s. 4d. So complete was their destruction by the reforming party that any that remain would be rarities indeed. A solitary specimen thought to have belonged to *Kilsby Church, Northampton,* is said to be owned by a Warwickshire gentleman. It is shaped like a coffer and measures 3 feet 9 inches long, 1 foot 3 inches wide, and 1 foot 9 inches high. Judging from the draping

---

* In 1549 the Sepulchre and frame for tapers thereto annexed was sold for xx^{d.}, and in 1561, xxvj^{s.} viij^{d.} was received for a sepulchre; the latter probably the one made in the reign of Queen Mary.

of the carved figures which ornament it, and particularly by the hood worn by Pilate, its execution has been assigned to the reign of Richard II., or the last twenty years of the fourteenth century. The cover is, comparatively speaking, modern.

The front is carved in relief in three square panels, 13 x 11 inches in size, and two similar panels adorn the ends, each containing a group of figures; the back, where it stood against the chancel wall, is plain. The panel at the easternmost end shows our Lord with hands bound, standing before Pilate, clad in a long tunic— the coat without seam,—the hood worn over the shoulders and in front of the breast, with a close-fitting cap on His Head. Of the five figures in the carving two are soldiers, one of whom is in knightly fourteenth-century armour. The western panel shows our Lord bearing His Cross, accompanied by a female, probably the Blessed Virgin Mary, and a soldier. The front of the coffer displays presumably, the Deposition from the Cross, the Resurrection, and the appearing to St. Mary Magdalene in the Garden—subjects identical with the carvings on several Easter Sepulchres.

Sir Roger Martin, of Melford Place, Suffolk, who was living at the time of the Reformation, in a manuscript on *Long Melford Church*, gives a description of such another timber sepulchre:

> " In the quire was a fair painted frame of timber to be set up about Maundy Thursday, with holes for a number of fair tapers to stand in before the Sepulchre, and to be lighted in service time. Sometimes it was set overthwart the quire before the High Altar, the Sepulchre being always placed and finely garnished at the north end of the High Altar; between that and Mr. Clopton's little chapel there is a vacant place of the wall, I think, upon the tomb of one of his ancestors; the said frame with the tapers was set near to the steps going up to the said altar. Lastly [*i.e.*, *latterly*], it was used to be set up along Mr. Clopton's aisle, with a door made to go out of the rood-loft into it."—Neale: *Views of Most Interesting Churches, &c.,* vol. ii.

The tomb alluded to is a rich canopied altar-tomb, with twelve niches above, once filled with statues of the Apostles, between the choir and the Clopton chapel, the north side of the chancel, the burial place of John Clopton, Esq., of Kentwell Hall, who died in 1497.

But the Easter Sepulchre belonging to the Church of *St. Mary Redcliffe, Bristol*, must surely have attained the height of perfection even of those mediæval days. The description is taken from an old document:

> "*Item*, that Maister Canyne hath delivered this 4th day of July, in the year of our Lord 1470, to Maister Nicholas Petters, Vicar of St. Mary Redcliffe, Moses Conterin, Philip Barthelmew, Procurators of St. Mary Redcliffe aforesaid, a new Sepulchre, gilt with golde, and a civer thereto. *Item*, an image of God Almighty, rising out of the same Sepulchre, with all the ordinance that longeth thereto, that is to say, a lathe made of timber and the ironwork thereto. *Item*, thereto longeth Heaven made of timber and stayned clothes. *Item*, Hell, made of timber thereto, with Divils to the number of thirteen. *Item*, four Knights armed, keeping the Sepulchre with their weapons in their hands; that is to say, two axes and two spears, with two paves [*i.e.*, shields]. *Item*, four payr of Angels' wings for four Angels, made of timber, and well painted. *Item*, the Fadre, the Croune, and Visage, the

Holy Ghost coming out of Heaven into the Sepulchre. *Item*, longeth to the four Angels, four chevelures [*i.e.*, perukes]."*

The fourth class of sepulchres are the imitations of the grave of Christ, and even of the church erected over it, which were much sought after in the early middle ages; all due in a great measure to the passion for Eastern warfare and pilgrimage which swept over Europe in the Crusades, and brought into being in 1118, the Order of Templars, to protect pilgrims to the Holy Sepulchre. These pilgrims often brought back the measurements expressly from Jerusalem, and the imitations appeared everywhere, the dedication of St. Sepulchre becoming very common. Somewhat later the holy sepulchre being introduced into the church itself, it took the form of the niche, or, still more rarely, of a separate chapel, as the one in the choir-corridor of the *Holy Cross Church, Gmund*, behind the high altar, in which the dead Christ is stretched out in an open sarcophagus, and surrounded by three sleeping watchmen, the two Marys, Mary Magdalene, and two angels. This work is of

---

* At Seville, a magnificent structure of wood, in three storeys, raised over the tomb of Father Columbus, and brilliantly lighted, serves as a sepulchre.

the 14th century, and is the favourite type followed in the succeeding period.

In the luxuriant architecture, called the Decorated and Perpendicular periods, which came in with the fifteenth century, these holy sepulchres developed into elaborate erections of stone with a wealth of carvings, ornamental canopied and tabernacle-work, as well as of symbolical detail. The finest specimens of such stone or marble structures, built for the express purpose of enshrining the Host in the sepulchre ceremony of Good Friday, remaining in England are those of *Lincoln Cathedral, St. Andrew, Heckington,* in the same county; *Northwold, Norfolk;* and *Patrington, Yorkshire.* The three former are of 14th century date, the latter a century older. All are one mass of pedimental pinnacled and canopied work, elaborately sculptured with the sleeping soldiers, the Maries, and rejoicing angels engaged in censing the rising Christ. At the entrance to the Sepulchre at Heckington, in addition to the censing angels surmounting it, angels kneel in adoration. In the Sepulchres at *South Pool* and *Woodleigh, Devon,* similar subjects are displayed: at the latter place they are the Descent from the Cross, the Resurrection, and the Visit of the Women to the Sepulchre, exactly identical with those carved on the portable Sepulchre at Kilsby.*

The fifth class of the Easter Sepulchre is the Sepulchre Chapel,—a chapel set apart and reserved for the ceremony. These were very rare and only to be found in cathedrals or large churches From the frescoes of the Birth, Life, Passion and Resurrection of Christ, which formerly covered the walls and vaulting of the chapel in the north wing (transept) of *Winchester Cathedral*, at the back of the choir stalls, it has been thought to have been associated with this practice. In *York Minster* (north side of nave towards the west end) was a Holy Sepulchre Chapel built by Bishop Roger.

The holy sepulchre being duly set up, its adornment was proceeded with. Hangings and curtains of rich brocade, silks, velvets, tapestries and cloths stained and painted with sacred story, were hung round about it, a canopy suspended over it, rich palls of work

---

* In the best example the form of the central structure is retained as in the 13th century example at *Constance*, in the chapel behind the quire, where in the centre of the octagon Gothic chapel stands a smaller octagon of stone in the genuine early Gothic form, ornamented on the exterior with the twelve Apostles, the Annunciation, Birth of Christ, Adoration of the Shepherds, and of the three Magian Kings; in the interior the sorrowing women at the grave and the sleeping watchmen are shown. In the *Dom at Mayence* the figures ornamenting the Easter Sepulchre are the size of life. See Lubkt, *Eccles. German Art.*

thrown over the sepulchre itself, while a veil of lawn or gossamer was drawn before it, to shield it in a measure from the view. From the early days it had been customary to cover the tombs or shrines of the saintly and the noble with such palls or veils of rich and costly material. A purple carpet covered the tomb of Cyrus; the veil from the tomb of St. Cæcilia was taken thence to subdue a conflagration; with the sacred carpet taken annually to Mecca to cover the tomb of the Prophet we are all familiar. Still earlier the Egyptians among other nations so covered their tombs and shrines of saints with palls. Many of the royal tombs at Westminster were so covered. Cnut's queen gave one for tomb of Edmund Ironside at Glastonbury, woven with figures of peacocks.

In the earliest account yet met with of the sepulchre (1214) mention is made of *velum unum de serico supra sepulchrum,* and in the later Parish Accounts numerous references are found to them. Thus for example:

1431. *London. St. Peter Cheap.*

"*Item,* j canapy steyned with iij staves and iiij boles of golde and iiij faynes (vanes?) and j clothe for the sepulcre steynede."

1457. *St. Michael, Cornhill.*

"*Item*, payd to Rote for ij whipps, iiij^d."*

37 Henry VI. *Bristol. St. Ewen* (destroyed).

"*Item*, paid for a batyment to hang a cloth on ye sepulchre in the chancel, ix^d. ob."

1557. *Bristol. Christ Church.*

"For a small corde to stay ye canabye over ye sepulcre."

At the Dissolution of *Westminster Abbey* there was a greate cove of bedde [tester-bed fashion] called a sepulchre cloth of nedlework.

1470. (10 Edward 4.) *London. St. Margaret Pattens.*

"*Item*, a Grete Cloth of Tapestri werke for to hang upon the walle by hynde the Sepulcur."

"*Item*, a Cloth of Sepulcur werke w^t the Ressurreccion the Passyon and w^t other werkis."

1485. *St. Margaret, Southwark.*

"*Item*, ij blew Cortyns [to] draw afore the sepulture."

---

* ? Pulleys for raising the canopy or pall veiling the sepulchre. The rope running over a pulley down into a ship's hold is called a "*whip*."

" *Item*, a lytyll Cortyn of grene sylke for the hede of the sepulture."

" *Item*, iij steyned Clothys with the Passyon and the Resureccyon to hang about the sepulture on good fryday."

1498. *St. Lawrence, Reading.*

" *Item*, a sepulcre cloth of right Crymson satten imbrowded w^t Image w^t a frontaill of pays conteyng in length iiij yards w^t ij cloths of lawnde for the sepulcre."

1527. *St. Mary Hill.*

" For painting and renewing the images in the sepulchre cloth, v^{s.}"

1550. (4 Edward VI.) *London. St. Dunstan in the East.*

" That that longes to the Sepulture and for good ffrydaye."

" *Item*, a Sepulture Cloth of cloth of golde."

" *Item*, a Canepye of cloth of golde w^t iiij stanes paynted Red belonging to the same."

" *Item*, a pece of whyte Sylke w^t iiij tasseles & iiij knappes of gold threde Lyke a Coverpane."

" *Item*, a pece of Sypres to Cary the Sacrament in."

" *Item*, a gerdle of Sylke w^t a Lyst of Blew and yelow."*

" *Item*, ij Napkyns for the high Aulter wroughte with sylke."

" *Item*, a shete to Laye in the Sepulture."

" *Item*, a greate Cossyn of Cloth of golde."

" *Item*, . . . an aulter cloth of the sepulture w^t Curtyns w^t Aunfelles."†

The inventory of 3 Edward VI. of *St. Dunstan in the East* show the sepulchre cloth there to have been of Cloth of Bawdkyn; at *St. Stephen's, Westminster*, of Cloth of Gold with red fygury and blue tynsyn. The inventories of the sixth year at *Ashford, Kent*, one of white sarcenet and two of green silk; at *All Saints, Canterbury*, red and blue chamlett; *St. Elphege*, " ij chaunge of hangynges "; *Lewisham* had three of linen and one of silk; at *Braborne* "a clothe of silke was used to be laid uppon the sepulcre." Of the two at *St. Christopher le Stock* " one was steyned with the Passion, the other full of white leves "; *St. Mary, Wimbledon*, had two of "cors clothe of gold "; at

---

* A similar entry appears in 1565, at *Wing, Bucks :* " *Item*, a pavlle for the Sepulcher of branchyde worke." " *Item*, a gyrdeyll off neiddle worke for the sepulcher."

† Public Record Office. *Ch. Gds. Exch.* Q. R. $\frac{4}{56}$.

Bucklebury, Berks, "ij paynted clothes wer wount to cover the sepulcre"; while at *Nattendon* in the same county, the sepulchre cloth was of black velvet with "a crose of Clothe of *Golde* wroughte Apon the same"; and at *Farley, Surrey,* of red and green silk. At *Sarratt* and *Hunsdon, Herts,* the clothes were of yellow silk popinjay.

Not infrequently rich articles of dress were bequeathed by will for this purpose, as the bequest of the wife of Lord Bardolph (Chamberlain to Henry VI.), who left by will to *Dennington Church, Suffolk,* "a purple gown with small sleeves to adorn the Easter Sepulchre there."

Frequent charges also appear in the accounts for "small cordes to the sepulchre," or for "whipcord to draw the curtin of the same sepulchre"; for "pynnys," "nailes," "greate tackes" and "sylke poynts" and "pack thred" to "pyne clotes" about it, and to keep the palls, etc., in place; likewise charges for dressing the Sepulchre,—the churchwardens of *Ludlow* in 1555-6 paying one Thomas Season "xij$^{d.}$ for thus 'dressing' the sepulchre." In the 31 Henry VI. the Churchwardens of *St. Margaret, Southwark,* paid five shillings for "lawne to the Sepulchre"; and again in 1485 appears an entry : " *Item*, iij Cortyns of lavnde [chlamide or lamine ?] to draw afore the sepul ture on the ester holy days."

It would seem from the inventories to have been customary in some instances to set carven angels either within or at the door of the sepul- chre after the Sacrament had been removed.

> 1431. *St. Peter Cheap.*
> " *Item*, j hersse for the sepulcre and iiij aungels thereto."
>
> 1485. *St. Margaret, Southwark.*
> " *Item*, vi angelles of tre [wood] gylt with a tombe to stande in the sepulture at Ester."
>
> 1511. (3 Henry VIII.) *St. Margaret Pattens.*
> " *Item*, twoo Angelles for the Sepulcre."

In the inventories of 1485 of *St. Mary's* (Benedictine Nunnery), *Langley, Leicestershire;* of 1552 (6 Ed. 6) of *Shenfilde, Berks*, and others, entries occur of " one fine shete for the sepul- cre," an item explained by the MS. inventory of *St. Dunstan in the East*, "a shete *to ly in* the sepulchre," *i.e.*, previous to the deposition of the Cross and Host.

As in mediæval times lights were lit about the graves of bishops and the shrines of saints on festivals,* so the Sepulchre was similarly illuminated, the tapers being supplied and maintained by general collection or individual gift. These lights were set upon and about the Sepulchre upon frames and beams of timber, or " lofts," as they were called at *St. Lawrence, Reading:*

> 1516. " Paid for makyng of the lofte for the sepulcre light, ij^{s.} ij^{d.}"
>
> 1538-9. " Payd for makeynge the beam lights on the sepulcre ayenst east ? xxj^{d.}"

In 1549 the Sepulchre and " frame for tapers thereto annexed " was sold, and in 1562 " the frame on which the Sepulcher Light did stand " was taken down with the Rood Loft.

These lights were tapers of wax, sometimes thirteen in number—to symbolise our Lord and His Apostles—every taper of six pounds weight, ' to burn around the Sepulchre at Passiontyde.' The chief among these was *the* ' Sepulchre Light,'—representing our Lord—in some instances of seventy-eight pounds weight, and rising to a height of thirty-six feet.

The *Sarum* rubrical direction was that one wax taper at least was to burn before the Sepulchre,

---

* *St. Gregory of Tours* speaks of it as a common practice in France in his day. *Perpetuus*, Bishop of Tours, 475, gave lands to maintain a light round St. Martin's tomb.

and the *Arbuthnot Missal* gives a like direction. In an inventory occurs the entry of "j candyl-stycke of yrne afore yᵉ sepulchre."* The *Constitutions* of the *Brigittine* nuns of *Syon* ordain only two tapers to burn 'in a more syker place for eschewing of perelle.'† At *Hereford* a lighted candle was to be placed within the Sepulchre with the Cross, and the door closed. ' Episcopus turificet sepulchrum et crucem, et accenso intus cereo claudat sepulchrum.' (*Harl. MS.* 2983.) At *Wells* the custom was similar, 'j cereus in sepulchro cum Corpore Dominico qui continue ardebit donec Matutinæ cantentur in die Paschæ.' (*MS. Harl.* 1682, *fo.* 5.) The Parish Accounts of *Ludlow* for 1557 have a like entry: "*Item*, to hym for makynge the toppe of one of them (sepulchre tapers) anewe after it was burnt out *in* the sepulcre, jᵈ." A quarter of a pound of wax being used to close the stok.

The monastic rule was : " Sit in unâ parte altaris, quâ vacuum fuerit, quædam assimilatis sepulchri, velamenque quoddum in extensum, in quo Sancta Crux deponatur in Parasceve et custodiatur usque dominicam noctem Resur-

---

* In 1552, *All Saints, Canterbury*, had two pillars to bear the sepulchre light.

† Aungier's *History of Syon*, p. 350.

rectionis, nocte verò ordinentur ij fratres aut iij aut plures qui ibidem palmos decantando excubias fideles exercent."—*Dugdale's Monasticon* i., p. 39, *compaɼe, Martene de Monast. Rituum* iv. 141.

The lamp in a tomb was a symbol of the rest of the righteous in a place of light, thus lamps were placed in the sepulchres of the martyrs buried in the catacombs; and the custom of hiding of the chief ' Tenebræ ' light behind the altar might go back to the time when the Cross or Host was buried there under the altar, one authority saying that the light so hidden was to abide there till Easter and be brought forth when Christ arose.

It is difficult to arrive at the general weight and proportion of these Sepulchre Lights, or the number employed. Probably there was no uniformity of practice, only one light being required, no restriction being laid upon the devout as to the number devotion might add for extra adornment. In the inventories the weight of wax employed is almost invariably reckoned up with that of the other church wax, *i.e.*, the making of the 'Paschal,' the 'font taper,' the ' cross ' and ' tenebræ ' candles. It seems a collection for providing these tapers and other Easter wax was made, and according to

the amount collected so the tapers were provided.* In the parish of *Wagtoft, Lincolnshire,*
there was an 'Alderman of the Sepulchre
Light,' whose duty it was doubtless to superin-
tend the collections for providing the light, or
to regulate the burning of the tapers, or the
'watching' at the Sepulchre. This was also
the case at *Thame, Oxon,* in 1465, where 'iii^{li}'
was received of the 'lightmen' of the Sepulchre; and at *Wing, Bucks,* in 1528, where 'ix$^{s.}$'
was "received of Wyllyam lukase & — Rafe
a burro lightman to the blessed sepulker."
The Holy Sepulchre at *Bury St. Edmund's*
appears to have been under the care of a guild,
as in 1463, John Baret bequeathed yearly 8$^{d.}$
for 8 tapers 'standyng at the grave of the
resurreccon gylde.'

In the parish of *Heybridge,* in the 21st year of
Henry VIII., the bachelors and maidens of the
parish provided the eighteen tapers — nine
apiece—each containing five pounds of wax,
belonging to the sepulchre, at the feast of
Easter. At *Stowmarket* also, and doubtless
other places, before the holy sepulchre, stood

---

* 1447. *St. Peter Cheap.* "*Item,* pade for a gal'on of wyne which
was yevyn to sypnam & to bogye for gederyng of money on good
frydaye, viijd. "

1521-2. *St. Andrew Hubbard.* "Receyved on good fryday toward
the sepulcre, iiijs. "

the 'Common Light,' and another known as the 'Bachelor's Light,' maintained at the cost of the single men of the parish.

These lights were also maintained by bequests, such as that left by *Thomas, Lord Dacre,* who left £100 to be employed towards the lights about the Sepulchre, in tapers of ten pounds weight each.* In the possession of the *Corporation of Bridport* is a document of the 15th year of Richard II., in which Robert Clement delivers twenty-five shillings, which he had "to find wax candles before our Lord's Sepulture."† Becon, in his *Acts of Christ and Antichrist,* says men give "twelve pence to the sepulchre light"

In 1485 at *St. Margaret's, Southwark,* four long cressets and four short ones were used " for to sett the lyghtss aboote the sepulture on good fryday, peynted rede with yrons to the same "; and in 1499 at *St. Mary Hill, London,* a payment for "a lampe and for tentyr hooks to the sepulchre," was made. In 1510 at *St. Andrew Hubbard's* there were three sepulchre tapers of eighteen pounds, and twenty-three shillings and seven pence received towards them; in 1535-7, seven shillings and eight

---

* *Test. Vetusta,* p. 653.
† Sixth Report of Historical MS. Commission, pt. 1, p. 476.

pence was collected and eight shillings expended. In 1552 at *Thame, Oxon*, twenty-two pence was received for two tapers. Three years later at *Ludlow* (an important parish), the taper cost six pence; the following year two tapers were bought for a shilling, and the next two "lyttle tapers" at the modest sum of two pence. The sepulchre at *St. Leonard's, Foster Lane*, in 1555 had sixteen tapers weighing twenty-four pounds at six shillings and eight pence; and that at *St. Michael's, Cornhill*, ten of two pounds of wax each.

This decrease in the number and weight of the candles was probably due in some measure by the appearance in 1538 of Henry the Eighth's (further) injunctions in which it was declared that none should "suffer from henceforth no candles, tapers, or images of wax, to be set before any image or picture, but only the light that commonly goeth about the cross of the church by the rood-loft, the light before the sacrament of the altar, and the light about the sepulchre."

On Easter Day the sepulchre was wont to be gloriously illuminated.*

---

* The Sepulchre at Norwich, like the one at Northwold, has an aperture for watching the light, without requiring the person so employed to enter the choir. The Church Accounts of *St. Ewen, Bristol* (1514), have the entry: "*Item*, for marchynge off the sepulchre lyght, viijd."

The Pyx containing the Host hanging over the altar was doubtless used very generally for the burial ceremony; but in some places as at *Poictiers*, the Host was wrapped in a folded corporal between two patens, with a gold cross above it, and then after being placed in clean linen, was enclosed with holy water and incense, within a repository, which was locked. In other, probably the more wealthy churches, a carven image or figure representing the dead or rising Christ in wood or one of the precious metals, in the breast of which was enclosed under beral (glass)* the Blessed Sacrament. Dugdale (*Monas. Angli.*) mentions such an one at *Lincoln Cathedral* of " silver and gilte, having a berale before, and a diamond behind," and others very similar were at *Durham* and *Wells.* In 1518, at *St. Peter Cheap, London*, were " iij Images for the Resurrexion." In 1552 (6 Edward 6) *St. Saviour's, Southwark*, had " ij peaces of silver knoppis which was in the breast of the ymage of the Resurrection "; and in the same year the Commissioners taking the inventory at *Greenwich*, endorsed a memorandum to the effect that all the goods in the inventory were delivered to the churchwardens

---

* *Leland*, in his account of Sudeley Castle, mentions as a thing to be noted, that some of the windows were glazed with BERAL.

save (*inter alia*) a "small thing of silver that stode in the brest of an Image of woode with a cristall stone, presented to be stolen." In 1557 the churchwardens of *Ludlow* made an entry "for makynge and kervynge the image for the resurrexion, xvij^d."

The Cross was laid upon a corporal spread within the Sepulchre.

Peacock, in his *English Church Furniture*, likewise mentions the destruction of such a Sepulchre Pyx at *Belton, in the Isle of Axholme, Lincolnshire:* "*Item*, a sepulker with little Jack broken in pieces one year ago [1565—6th Elizabeth]; but little Jack was broken in pieces this year [1566] by the said churchwardens." This 'little Jack' so irreverently referred to was the repository of the Blessed Sacrament, and may have been fashioned as a man like the instances above mentioned.

On the contrary the 1552 Commissioners found at *All Saints, Canterbury,* "a litill monstros of sylver clene gylte for the resurrection."

As to the actual burial of the Host a fifteenth century MS. tells us that according to the *Sarum Use*—a Use which for some time before the Reformation had practically superseded all others—the procession was to go through the west door to the place of the first station, on the north side of the church, where the priest put off his 'chesible' and took the Cross with feet unshod and in his surplice, and deposited it in the Sepulchre, and afterwards the Host in a Pyx.

> 1517. *St. Andrew Hubbard, East Cheap.*
>
> "*Item*, paid to a prest ffor berrying of the sakkerment, ij^{d}."

> 37 Henry VI., *St. Ewen, Bristol.*
>
> "For berying of the sepulchre, ij^{d}."

It may be well to insert here an instance of what was probably a Sepulchre with its appurtenances complete :

> 1466. *London. St. Stephen, Coleman Street.*
>
> "*Item*, the resurrecon of our lorde w^{t} the avyse in his bosn to put the sac'ment therein."
>
> "*Item*, anothir grete branch be for the Resurrecon in . . . .   w^{t} v small branches ther'on."
>
> "*Item*, xxij'th disshes for the sepulcur' and ij disshes for the pascalle w^{t} Cordes that ptainis thereto."
>
> "*Item*, j grete glasse hangng be for the resurreccon in the chaunsell."

"*Item*, j sepulcur' on gyldyd, wᵗ j frame to be set on wᵗ iiij poste and cryste 'p to."

"*Item*, iiij trestell to have the sepult' downe wᵗ iiij ironys to be'r hᵗ vp wᵗ."

"*Item*, iiij Angell for to be set on the posts wᵗ iiij sencs 'ij gyldyd and ij not gylgyt."

"*Item*, iiij grete angell to be set on the sepulcur' wᵗ dyu's small angell."

"*Item*, ij steyned clothes wᵗ the apostoll and the ppete bettyn wᵗ golde wᵗ the crede'."

"*Item*, viij bar'es bettyn wᵗ golde to be set abowte the sepulcur' wᵗ dyus small pyns."

"*Item*, iiij knyghte to be set on the poste befor the do'r."

"*Item*, j angyll to be set in the do'r."

"*Item*, j canape steyned wᵗ a son of Golde to heng on the sepulcur' at ester'."

"*Item*, j Rydyl (canopy) steyned wᵗ a chalix and the fygur' of the sacrament on hyt."

1542. "*Item*, a clothe to drawe on the sepulture."

After the deposition of the Sacrament a constant succession of worshippers of all classes kept watch before It, " in reparation for the watching of the perfidious Jews and blind heathen round our Lord's sepulchre of humilia-tion in Jerusalem." At *Lichfield* three persons kept unbroken vigil and sang psalms until mattins were said on Easter morning. At *Poictiers* five watchers guarded the sepulchre. At *Trinity Church, Coventry,* in 1452, the second deacon was to watch the sepulchre on the night of Easter Eve, and the first deacon on Good Friday all night.* *Moleon* says the watchers at *Orleans,* habited as soldiers, broke their lances before the third stall [at the close of the watching] in the presence of the chanter, and marched round the church with bare swords, and the sub-deacon began the *Te Deum.* Usually there were two or three watchers who maintained the watch, and numer-ous items relative to this watching appear in the parish accounts and inventories:

> 1480-2. *London. St. Andrew Hubbard, East Cheap.*
>
> " *Item,* paid for brede ale and fyre to watche the sepulcre, vj$^{d.}$"
>
> 1517. " *Item,* paid ffor ij watchers of the sepulker, viij$^{d.}$"; ffor choles† & alle & brede, vij$^{d.}$"

---

* Constitutions of Office of Trinity Church, Coventry.

† Coles, always *charcoal*—" colis to sense with "

1526-7. "Paid at Ester for Colis bred drynke and for a man to watche the sepulcre."

1532. *London. St. Peter Cheap.*
" *Item,* p'd for watchyng on goode frydaye & on Easter Evyn & for drynke for the watchers, xij[d.]"

1538. *St. Margaret's, Westminster.*
" For mats for the parishioners to kneel upon when they reverenced their Maker, iiij[s.] iiij[d]"

1555. (26 Hen. VIII.) *St. Peter Cheap.*
" *Item,* paide for watchynge the sepulcre at easter and for brede and drynke for them that watched, ij[s.]"
" *Item,* for ij sakkes of coles for the watchmen and to make ffyer w[t] all on Easter Eve, xviij[d.]"

1558. *Reading. St. Mary's.*
" Paid to Roger Brock, for watching of the sepulchre, viij[d.]"
" Paid more to the saide Roger for syses [candles-sixes] and collis, iij[d.]"

2. Edward VI. " *Item,* for watching the sepulchre, viij[d.]; for frankincense, iij[d.]"

This watching was continued without intermission until the Mattins of Easter. Barnabe

Googe in 1570, thus describes "the Resurrection of the Lord."*

"At midnight then with carefull minde, they up to mattens rise,
  The clarke doth come, and after him, the Priest with staring eies :
  The Image and the breade from out the graue (a worthie sight)
  They take, and Angels two they place in vesture white.

  .   .   .   .

  In some place solemne sightes and showes, and pageants fayre are
    play'd,
  With sundry sortes of maskers braue, in straunge attire aray'd,
  As where the Maries three doe meete, the sepulchre to see,
  And John with Peter swiftly runnes, before him there to bee."

The author of the *Durham Rites* thus describes the ceremony as it occurred there : "There was in the Abbey Church of Durham, very solemn service upon Easter Day, betwixt three or four of the clock in the morning in honour of the Resurrection, where two of the eldest monks of the quire came to the Sepulchre, set up on Good Fryday after the Passion, all covered with red velvet and embroider'd with gold, and did then cense it, either of the monks with a pair of censers, sitting on their knees before the sepulchre.   Then they both rising came to the sepulchre, out of which with great reverence they took a marvellous beautiful image of our Saviour, representing the Resurrection, with a Cross in His hand ; in the breast whereof was enclosed, in the most bright

---

* *Popish Kingdom.*

chrystal, the Sacrament of the Altar, through which chrystal the Blessed Host was conspicuous to the beholders. Then after the elevation of the said picture carried by the said two monks, upon a fair velvet cushion all embroider'd, singing the anthems of *Christus Resurgens*, they brought it to the high altar, setting it on the midst thereof, and the two monks kneeling before the altar, and censing it all the time that the rest of the whole quire were singing the foresaid antheme of *Christus Resurgens;* which antheme being ended, the two monks took up the cushion and picture from the altar, supporting it betwixt them, and proceeding in procession from the high altar to the south quire door, where there were four ancient gentlemen belonging to the Prior, appointed to attend their coming, holding a most rich canopy of purple velvet, tassell'd round about with red silk and a goodly gold fringe; and at every corner of the canopy did stand one of these ancient gentlemen to bear it over the said images, with the Holy Sacrament carried by the monks round about the church, the whole quire waiting upon it with goodly torches, and great store of other lights; all singing and praising God, till they came again to the high altar."*

---

* *Durham Rites*, Surtees Society, pp. 10, 11.

Martene De Antiquis Monachorum Ritibus (1590) also treats of "De Resurrectione Dominica."

In the various Uses throughout England and Scotland similar rites were prescribed, and generally a separate procession for the Host and the Cross from the Sepulchre.*

In earlier times, as Barnabe Googe says, this '*Office of the Sepulchre*' took the form of the Mystery Play (or was performed by puppets), when three deacons, representing the three Marys, the priest as the risen Christ, and a boy as an angel performed, the part taking place at the Resurrection of our Lord in the Garden, for which see Du Cange, v. *Sepulchri Officium*, and Martène, *De Antiquis Monachorum Ritibus*, and Migne *Patrologia*, cxlvii., 139.

The Household book of the fifth Earl of Northumberland, for the year 1512, mentions this practice :

> "*Item* . . to them   that play the play of Resurrection upon Estur day in the mornnynge in my lordis 'chappell' befor his lordshipe, xx^{s.}" (Sect. xliv. p. 345.)

---

* 1555. Ludlow. "Paid for ij lynkes at Ester to bere before the sacrament, xxd."

At *Witney, Oxford,* the Resurrection of our Lord was set forth yearly after the manner of a show or interlude. The acting of plays in churches lingered on after the Reformation, the only difference being that profane stories took the place of the religious. Parish clerks always took the principal share and parts in the representation of the ' mysteries.' One of the chief players in this puppet-play of the Resurrection was one of the watchmen who, seeing Christ arise, made a continuous noise, like the meeting of two sticks, and was therefore named Jack Snackes. The Rood of Witney was called ' Jack Knacker of Witney,' probably from this circumstance.* *Cardinal de Joyeuse,* Archbishop of Rouen, abolished the ceremonial, as in France it had been profaned by attempts at positive personation.

About the year 1543, the rites and ceremonies of the English Church were brought under review, and a Rationale drawn up to explain the meaning and justify the usage. In this the rites of the Easter Sepulchre are stated and expounded as follows

" And that day [Good Friday] is prepared and well adorned the sepulchre in remembrance of His Sepulchre, which was prophesied by the

---

* Lambarde's *Topographical Dictionary,* 1570.

prophet Esaias to be glorious, wherein is laid the image of the cross, and the most blessed Sacrament, to signify that there was buried no corpse or body that could be purified or corrupted, but the pure and undefiled body of Christ, without spot or sin, which was never separated from the Godhead. And therefore, as David expresseth in the fifteenth Psalm, it could not see corruption, nor death could not detain, or hold Him, but He should rise again to our great hope and comfort; and therefore the Church adorns it with lights, to express the great joy they have of that glorious triumph over death, the devil, and hell.

"Upon Easter Day in the morning, the ceremonies of His resurrection are very laudable, to put us in remembrance of Christ's resurrection, which is the cause of our justification. And that as Christ being our head, was the first among the dead which rose never to die again; so all Christian men being His members, do conceive thereby to rise from death of sin to godly conversation in this life; and finally, at the day of judgment, when the bodies and flesh of all mankind shall by the operations of God be raised again, to rise with Him to everlasting glory."*

---

* See Collier, vol. v., pp. 106-24.

This devotion of the Sepulchre survived the so-called Reformation of King Henry the Eighth, continuing to be observed in the early years of the reign of Edward the Sixth, the Sepulchre remaining at *Ludlow* in 1548 after the Rood and images had been taken down. On Easter Day, at *Worcester* (March 15th, 1548—2nd Edward VI.), 'the Pyx, with the Sacrament in it, was taken out of the Sepulchre, they singing " Christ is risen," with procession, and all this when on Palm Sunday no palms were hallowed and on Good Friday there was no creeping to the Cross.'*

In the reign of Mary an attempt was made to restore the old condition of things, but her death and the accession of Elizabeth again placed them in the position they occupied in the early years of Edward VI.'s reign, when many of the ancient usages and devotions, that of the Easter Sepulchre among them, fell into total desuetude.

Now-a-days, among the followers of the Roman Rite, the devotion of the Sepulchre taking a ñew development, has been transferred to the adoration at the Altar of Repose on Maundy Thursday, which is somewhat of an anachronism, seeing that this so-called burial

---

* Green's *History of Worcester*, vol. i., p. 127.

precedes the death of Christ on Good Friday, which has no connection whatever with the Thursday, but so popular was this Sepulchre ceremony that even now it has retained its name in the minds of the people, and liturgical writers have even adopted it.

Altogether this is a very interesting point, *i.e.*, the difference between the Sepulchre and the Altar of Repose. The oldest rubrics to which I have reference order the reservation to be made in the usual place, that is to say, in the Hanging Pyx over the High Altar, and later (16th century) in the Tabernacle. In the earlier times of tabernacles it would seem to have been necessary to reserve at a secondary altar, because it was not considered proper to say Mass at any altar at which the Blessed Sacrament was in reservation.* Hence probably arose the custom of preparing a secondary altar on Maundy Thursday, which would naturally lead to the custom of providing some special place or Réposoir. Then by way of simplification (?) they began to combine this with the Sepulchre, as did the *Benedictines* of *St. Maur.* Anciently the *Cistercians* had neither Réposoir nor Sepulchre, though they had the

---

* The Catholic Apostolic Church (Irvingites) always remove the reserved Sacrament from the altar previously to a celebration.

hanging Pyx; the *Carthusian Ordinarium* expressly forbids either, as a secular custom incompatible with their 'solitude.' The *Missal of Bayeux* (1642) distinguishes the two reservations, one, 'Hostia,' is to be reserved for the morrow—the other is to be 'adored in the Sepulchre,' with the cross.

The Greeks have a very similar rite to that of the western Easter Sepulchre. On Good Friday the Archimandrite, after reading that part of the Gospel which tells how Pilate delivered Christ to be crucified, brings from the Sanctuary a large crucifix, and places it in the centre of the Church, and the representation of the burial of Christ takes place in a grave in the shape of a mausoleum in the centre of the Church, and the 'Lamentations' are sung in a very impressive manner. In some places the effigy (or a painting on white satin) is borne through the streets upon a bier as if going to burial, preceded by priests, choristers, and funeral music, the people following behind in great numbers, carrying lighted tapers.

Even among the heathen was performed a kindred ceremony—a figure or symbol of what was to come. The myth of the Phœnicians was nearly akin to those of Chaldea. Adonis-Thammuz, beloved by the goddess Baalath

(Beltis in the Greek), was killed by the tusk of a fierce boar, hunting—implying the victory of the fierce and wicked sin-god, the Destroyer, over the beneficial sun, the fair spring god, the bridegroom of Nature in her prime—and coming to life again. The festival was celebrated in early spring, and began in mourning. A procession of wailing women, tearing their hair and clothes, cried aloud that the god was dead; calling upon his name, they repeated, " Woe is us ! " They laid a wooden effigy of him, clothed in regal robes, on a bier, anointed it with oil, and performed over it the other rites for the dead, fasting severely all the while. The bier carried in procession was followed by an ever-increasing crowd with every demonstration of grief. Afterwards the god's resurrection was celebrated with equally extravagant rejoicings, the air resounding with the triumphant cry of " Adonis is living."

The Great Paschal.

THE hallowing or blessing of the Great Paschal or Easter Candle, and previously of the New Fire with which it was afterwards lighted, was the chief ceremonial observance of the Vigil of Easter.

Taking it as a general rule there can be little doubt that the earlier Holy Saturday ceremonies as well as the other observances of the Holy Week, including much of the older Palm Sunday ceremonial, were copied in the West from the East, having had their origin either at Jerusalem or Antioch. At the former, as is generally known, the ceremony of obtaining new fire in the church of the Holy Sepulchre is still practised, and which was originally doubtless nothing more than something akin to the present Western rite, although it has become to be regarded by the ignorant as miraculous; as at one time the lamps of the Holy Sepulchre church were pretended to be miraculously lighted upon this day,—called by the Copts and Mooslims *Sebt en Noor,* or Saturday of the Light.

The kindling of fire upon an altar was the most sacred of religious ceremonies, and a custom much more prevalent in ancient times than it is now. The Roman Vestals maintained such a sacred fire in their temples,—for the Shrines of Vesta had no statues of that goddess, her presence being represented by the eternal fire, fabled to have been brought by Æneas from old Troy. So also the Peruvian Virgins of the Sun, and the Parsees. The sacred fires of the Saxon temples were not extinguished till the arrival of Saint Augustine, and the perpetual, jealously-guarded light in the fire-house of Saint Bridget of Kildare burned unquenched from the fifth to the thirteenth century (1220).*

The most primitive method of kindling this fire (which was restricted to a priest) was by the means of a glass from the sun or by producing it anew by friction out of two peculiarly-shaped pieces of wood, called in

---

* In the Life of St. Patrick it is told how he kindled an Easter-fire, on Easter Eve, A.D. 433, on the hill of Slane, standing opposite Tara. Rustics of Pourrières (*Campi Putridi*) still celebrate a yearly festival, at which they burn a vast heap of brushwood on the summit of a hill, shouting Victoire! Victoire! in memory of Marius.

the Indian religions Ashvattha-wood, and known to us as the "fylfot" cross, the crooked ends being handles by which two sticks were worked about a common axle till it burst into flame. *See* 1 *Kings* xvii. 12. Around the altars found in Denmark, Sweden and Norway, stones for striking fire were found, for no other fire except such as was struck forth from a flint was pure enough for so holy a purpose as the perpetual fire which burned before the Scandinavian altars. When the Vestal Virgins had allowed their sacred fire—the old hearth fire of the Latin tribe settled at Rome—to expire, they rekindled it by means of a mirror from the sun; so also in the great golden sun temples, the virgin guardians drew new fire from heaven at the great festival of the summer solstice, called the feast of raymi, by means of a concave mirror From the sun the Anglo-Saxons caught the first spark of fire on tow for their day service by means of a strong burning glass; if cloudy, they produced it from a flint. At the winter solstice the northern nations celebrated the birthday of the new sun by kindling new fire.*

---

* *Quintus Curtius* (Lib. iii. c. 3), describing the march of a Persian army, says that on the top of the tent of the king was placed an image of the sun in crystal, and that the holy fire was borne on silver altars.

Many of our Christian ceremonies are known to have had their origin in the rites of the heathen, and doubtless much of the ceremonial practised on the heathen festival kept in honour of the sun, after being sanctified by the Church, became grafted upon our Easter celebration. Easter was of old the first day of the Christian new year, and on its eve every spark of fire, both in religious and secular use, was devoutly extinguished, to be rekindled by the new, blessed by the Church.

In fact, this rite of blessing new fire, as of the Paschal, is, beyond doubt, nothing less than the crystallisation of a rite formerly universally practised, not alone on the Vigil of Easter, but either every day, or at least every Saturday, namely, the custom of blessing and lighting a candle or lamp, or a number of either, a practice very similar to the Jewish rite of ceremonially lighting the Tabernacle lamps, as mentioned in the first book of Samuel.

In support of this we have, among other things, the Greek Canon 39 of *Con. Illele* (ca. 320), and further, the hymns of *Prudentius Clemens* (d. 405), entitled "*Ad incensum cerei paschalis*," written with reference to the daily lighting up for Vespers or the Lucernarium, and had no connection with the hymn, " *Inventor rutili*," which was commonly sung during the office of the benediction of the Easter taper, and which is quoted as an argument for the antiquity of the rite, being in fact only an excerpt of forty lines from a much longer hymn, which, according to the best reading, is properly entitled *ad incensum lucernæ* —at the lighting of the lamp—and not *de cereo paschali.* Being No. V. of the *Cathemerinon* hymns, this was clearly intended for daily use at the Vesper service, when candles were wont to be solemnly lighted.

About the year 1100 the custom would appear to have been reserved exclusively for Holy Saturday, and concentrated into one yearly instead of weekly ceremony, appropriately significant of the rising again of the " Light of Light like the Sun in His strength."*

The Acts of the *Fourth Council of Toledo* mention that it was customary to bless candles for Vespers every evening, and that on Holy Saturday the benediction was particular and solemn, the candle being bigger than usual for the simple reason that it was to burn all night. This custom of blessing candles persisted in

---

* *Chaucer*, quoting St. Isidore, makes his Parson tell of anger: that like a fire it will last a year or more—from one Easter-day until another Easter-day.

Ireland till the end of the seventh century, whereas the *Gallican Liturgies* of the same period have already the Paschal Candle and it alone.

Anciently in England this hallowing of new fire was not confined, as now, to Holy Saturday, but was performed on each of the three last days of Holy Week,* a custom which was preserved in monastic churches, when it had otherwise been transferred into one of benediction of fire on Easter Eve in connection with the " Benedictio Cerei." Thus according to the *Rites* of *Durham* the great Paschal is said to have burned from Maundy Thursday till the Wednesday after Ascension Day, and the *Cluniac* custom was to the same effect: " If any one would celebrate mass on Holy Thursday, before the Solemn mass was sung, he made no use of light, because the new fire was not yet blessed.† At *Auch* (Missal 1491), new fire was struck from a flint and blessed before the altar on Maundy Thursday after None. In an XIth century MS. (Vat. Cod. lat. 4772) is preserved another form of blessing

---

* Roughly speaking, it seems the office of the three last days of Holy Week preserve the original form of the daily service, glorified of course for the special solemnity.

† Stevens' translation of the French *History of the Monastic Orders.*

fire on Maundy Thursday with a rubric directing that a lamp or candle is to be lit from it, and that from this again are to be kindled the Paschal fire and candles (*cerei*) on Easter Eve.* According to an Albi Sacramentary,† on Holy Saturday the great Paschal was to be lighted from the fire " quod V feria de silice et xpistallo excussus fuerit." On Holy Saturday (and presumably on Good Friday also) the new fire was blessed (with the prayer " *Deus qui Moysi famulo tuo,*") and the incense as on Maundy Thursday. The Missal of 1555 (printed at Toulouse) says new fire was blessed after *Mandatum* on Maundy Thursday. Even as late as the eighteenth century in some of the more strict of the monastic houses the new fire was not hallowed till six or seven in the evening. *Rabanus Maurus,* describing the ceremonies of Holy Saturday, at the commencement of the ninth century, says, there was no morning mass, but as the evening drew on (*die inclinante ad vesperam*) began the blessing of the Paschal Candle, the long prayers and baptisms. At *Salisbury* it took place after None.

---

* Vide *Quellen und Forschungen zur Geschichte und Kunstge-schicte Des Missale Romanum im Mittelalter. Iter Italicum,* von Dr. Adalabert Ebner. Freiburg. Herder. Quoted by a Writer in *Dublin Review* or *Month,* vol. 1896.

† MS. VI. Town Hall, Albi.

According to present Western use the ceremony takes place in the day-time, though some
parts of the office would infer (as was the case)
that they were anciently performed in the night-
time, when the faithful were gathered together
watching for the dawning of Easter morning,
and probably before the celebration of the
midnight or first Easter Day Eucharist—
the Vigil having anciently had the name of
lucernariæ preces or *gratiarum actiones*, the
prayer and thanksgiving of lamp light.

Giraldus, writing in the twelfth century,
says: " In Sabbato magno circa *noctis initium,*"
(celebratur missa) *; which shows that in his
time they took place late in the afternoon. At
Canterbury, on the contrary, we read the
convent in albes singing the *Miserere*, assembled
on the morning of Easter Eve to watch the
kindling of the flame by the deacon.

Anciently it was customary to bless many
secular things—houses, ships, first fruits, the
bridal-bed, &c.—so on this day all lights and
fires having been extinguished, were relighted
with fire newly blessed, a survival of which is
still seen in the distribution of the new fire in
the Church of the Holy Sepulchre at Jerusalem,
upon this day. The author of the " *Popish*

---

* *Gemma Eccles.* p. 24. (Rolls Edition.)

Kingdom" says that men took home brands of the new fire.*

Previously to the "hallowing" of the new fire all lights throughout the church were extinguished, (at Sext, to be relighted practically at None), on account of the eclipse of the sun during those hours of the "agony."† In cathedral and conventual churches the ceremony was performed in the east alley of the cloister, though at *Salisbury* it seems to have taken place at the pillar to the south of the font—and in parish churches in the porch. It is doubtful whether the ceremony was observed in all churches, perhaps only in the larger and better appointed ones.

The new fire was brought into being according to the ancient method from the sun by means of a burning glass or crystal, as a type of the "Orient on high." At *Cluny* a precious beryl was employed. *Leo IV.* in the ninth century mentions it as being produced from a flint, (symbolical of the Rock—1 *Cor.* x. 4).‡ At *Florence*, a flint brought from Jerusalem in the time of the Crusades was used.

---

* *In France* the First Sunday in Lent is called from the ancient ceremonial, Sunday in Brandons (torches), or of Hearths; in *Germany* Spark Sunday.

† *Gemma Animæ*, p. 1280.

‡ The Blessing of Fire was unknown in Rome in the time of Pope Zacharius (751).

Rupert, Abbot of Deutz, c. 1111, in chapter " De novo igne," says : " Amisso igne, qui ad matutinos   extinguitur, ad lapidem per eosdem tres dies confugimus, ut vel lapidem percutientes, ex abstrusis ejus venis ignem occultum eliciamus, vel liquidum crystalli lapidem sereno coelo soli objicientes, radium ejus trajectum per ejusdem crystalli orbiculum spectabili miraculo in subjectam suscipiamus escam." (*De Divinis Officiis;* lib. v. cap. 28.)

In 924, in some ritual customs which *St. Ulric,* bishop of Augsburg, set forth, and adopted afterwards by the *Cluniac* monks, a semi precious stone or beryl was employed and carried in the holy Saturday procession. It was probably a fine large piece of rock crystal mounted in a frame of gold or silver, " lapis pretiosus berillus in quo ignis est producendus.* The Parish Accounts of *St. Peter's, Cheap,* for the year 1555 have an entry for "coles [charcoal] to make ffyre w^t all on Easter Eve." *Hospinian* thus refers to the consecration of the Paschal :—

" Cereus hinc ingens, Paschalis dictus, amœno
  Sacratur cantu ; cui ne mysteria desint,
  Thurea compingunt in facta foramina grana."

---

* *Rock,* p. 98, vol. 3, pt. 2. The earliest mention of procuring the new light from flint and steel is said to occur in an Homily of Leo IV. (*De Cur. Pastor,* c. 7), middle of 9th century. *Rupertus Tuitiensis,* c. 1111, leaves the procuration optional by either glass or flint and steel.

The fire being kindled and blessed, the sacristan lighted a taper,—generally three tapers branching from a common stock set on the top of a lance-like staff was used. In some places the upper candle of the Tenebræ was reserved for the purpose, in others as at Rome, in 750, in the pontificate of Zozimus, three lamps, which had been concealed in token of the three days in which the Redeemer lay in the tomb.* In some place the light when kindled was placed in a lantern attached to a lance or wand, as we read : The master of the boys having kindled his lantern, the procession, often led (in cathedral churches) by the primate with incense and cross returned to the quire chanting the hymn " Inventor rutili," the deacon announcing *Lumen Christi*, the Light of Christ, three times, whilst (in monastic houses) the servant of the cellarer rekindled, with the fire remaining in the cloister, all the hearths which had previously been extinguished, and the people took home brands of the holy fire, as formerly at Rome, and in pre-Reformation times in England, to rekindle all the cold hearths of village, town, and city. In other uses the Precentor or *Magister Schole* at

---

* Three lamps at Durham were similarly extinguished on Good Friday.

the appointed time sang out thrice in a loud voice "Accendite," and thereupon the whole church was illuminated.

Between this rite and that of the blessing of candles at Candlemas there doubtless exists an intimate relation. In fact, a taper was preserved from the Candlemas blessing, of bleached wax, for the ceremonial benediction of fonts on the Eves of Easter and Whitsuntide. Moreover, another authority adds that the Candlemas tapers were lighted by fire kindled by the bishop. According to *Dr. Rock** there used to be two distinct blessings at Candlemas, one over the unlighted wax tapers, the other over the fire, (most likely a burning candle), from which afterwards all others were lit.

This rekindling of new fire represented both the resurrection of the Lord and the fire which He came to cast upon the earth (*St. Matt.* xii. 49).

The origin of the Paschal Candle is lost in obscurity. It is certainly not mentioned before the fifth century, but can be traced back to the sixth. Its institution is attributed by some to Pope Zozimus (417) on the strength of the notice in his life in the *Liber Pontificalis*, "per parochias concessa licentia cereos benedicti,"

---

* *Church of Our Fathers*, vol. iv., p. 60.

or according to another version, "per parochias concessit ut cereos benedicerent"; but
*Baronius** points out that this really implies an
extension to parish churches of a custom
already existing in (probably) the great basilicas.
Becon† says Zozimus ordered its hallowing
in 414, and adds, some make Pope Theodorus
author of it (613).

Nevertheless it has a most venerable tradition
of ancient usage, as *St. Jerome* (in his Epistles)
and *St. Augustine* (in "De Civitate Dei,"
xv. 22) both allude to it—the latter saying "in
laude quandam cerei breviter versibus, dixi,"
etc., where "cerei" and not "creatoris" seems
the true reading. The most ancient of "Sacra-
mentaries," that of *St. Gelasius* (495), has the
solemn blessing for it inserted, and *Eunodius*,
Bishop of Pavia (519)‡ has left two forms of
benediction.§ From an expression in one of
these it may be inferred that the practice of
preserving particles of wax from the taper as
charms had already grown up. *St. Gregory
the Great*‖ and Canon ix. of the *IV. Council of*

---

* *Annales* in ann. 418.

† *Reliques of Rome,* 164. *Quoting Isidor Volat, Platina. D. Barus,*
and *Chron. Fasciculus, Temporum.*

‡ Bishop of Ticino? (d. 521).

§ Eunodii, Op. tom. 1, "*Cura Sirmondi.*"

‖ *Epist.* xi. 33.

Toledo (633), both speak clearly of the Paschal taper and its blessing. *Durandus* says St. Ambrose made the benediction or prayer for hallowing, and, moreover, that Augustinus and Petrus Diaconus the monk made also other benedictions, which are not in use.*

Moreover, we have the testimony of the permanent constructional Paschal (or Gospel) Candlesticks attached to the ambons of the ancient Roman basilican churches. Yet for all this the custom would appear not to have been a Roman one, but one of Spanish origin, spreading northwards from that country, and being adopted at Rome (perhaps by Pope Theodore), the candle being set upon a column, which thus recalled the more ancient column of wax, upon which was written the *Breve Anni.*

The ancient Spanish form of benediction included the prayer, " May our souls be lamps of Thine, kindled and illuminated by Thee, may they shine and burn with the truth and never go out in darkness and ashes."

Anciently the Great Paschal or Easter Candle gave light during the watching in the church on Easter Eve in the night-time, and thus necessarily it was of great size. In later times it varied from three to three hundred pounds in

---

* *Rationale divinorum Officiorum.*

weight, though from ten to twenty pounds would seem to have been its general weight. Sometimes it was made of thirty-three pounds of wax, in allusion to the number of years of our Lord's earthly life. In some few of the great and wealthy churches it assumed the colossal proportions of three hundred pounds weight, as at *Westminster Abbey Church, Canterbury Cathedral* in 1457, and at the *Abbey Church of Durham,* where it towered up to within a man's length of the roof, from whence it was lighted. From a similar height also the candle was lighted at *Norwich,* where the orifice remains. At *Coutances* it was lighted from the clerestory; at *St. John Lateran, Rome,* by a deacon, wheeled up in a portable pulpit for the purpose ; while at *Seville* a chorister climbed up a gilt iron rod, furnished with steps like a flag-staff, with the top railed in, whence he lights the candle, drawing off the melted wax with a large iron ladle. The church of *St. Stephania, Naples,* was burned down by fire caught from the Paschal candle on Easter night, during which it was the local custom, in the eighth century, to leave it unextinguished.*

---

* The great height of many of these candles was due in a measure to the gigantic, and in many instances, magnificent candlesticks whereon they were set.

On the other hand we find the Paschal taper at *Lincoln Cathedral,* only a modest three pounder, while at *Evesham Abbey* they seem to have dispensed with it altogether, as do the *Carthusians* who have no " new fire " on Holy Saturday, and no Paschal.

Merati says it is a rubrical injunction that the weight of this waxen taper should be from eight to ten pounds: yet the Paschal at *Rheims* weighed thirty pounds; at *Chartres,* seventy-two pounds; and at *Rouen,* forty pounds, and at the latter place was twenty-five feet in height. At *Seville,* at the beginning of the present century, it weighed 2,000 lbs. of twelve ounces, nine yards high and thick in proportion.*
The English rule of the Paschal being thirty-six feet in height, originally referred to *Sarum Cathedral* only.

The general weight of the Paschal is somewhat difficult to arrive at in consequence of other church wax,—the font taper, the cross candle, the trendal, the tenebræ tapers, etc.,—being thrown in with it, *e.g. :—*

> 1554. *London. St. Michael, Cornhill.*
> " Paide for the Sepulker Lyght at Easter & for the Pascall & for the Tenebar candles, vij$^{s.}$ vj$^{d.}$ "

---

* Blanco White (Leucadis Doblado), Letters from Spain, p. 299.

1555. "Paide for the Paskall with the Crosse candels, & ij$^{lis.}$ of Tenebar candles weiyinge all vij$^{lis.}$ at xi$^{d.}$ a pounde vj$^{s.}$ v$^{d.}$"

1 Ed. VI. *Bristol. St. Ewen* (destroyed). The Paschal, font, taper, and other wax came to x$^{s.}$ ix$^{d.}$ ob.

In 1447 at *Thame, Oxon*, the Paschal was about 2 lbs.; in 1534-5, 4$\frac{1}{4}$ lbs. at two shillings and seven pence. In 1478 at *St. Mary Hill, London*, 30 lbs. In 1508 at *St. Lawrence, Reading*, it was 20 lbs., at eight shillings and fourpence; at *Ludlow* for the years 1540-9 it varied between .7 and 16 lbs., and in the years 1555-8 from 5 to 13 lbs. at a cost also varying between five shillings and thirteen shillings and five pence. At *St. Peter Cheap, London*, in 1555, it was of 8 lbs., as it was at *Heybridge* in the reign of Henry VIII., and in the sixth year of Edward VI., at *St. Leonard's, Foster Lane*, it was of no more than 5 lbs. weight.

The churchwardens' accounts show a general levy was made upon the parishioners just before Easter, (sometimes on Good Friday), for money or wax towards the paschal and other Easter wax. The usual "Offering days" were Christmas, Easter, Whitsuntide, and the

feast of Dedication, or as *Beleth* says, All
Saints, when the alms were allotted for the
priest's stipend and the purchase of the paschal.
The Laws of the Danish.king Cnut, ordered
tribute of " Light scot thrice in the year.
First on Easter Eve, a $\frac{1}{2}$d. worth for every hide
[of land], and again on all hollows mass as
much; and again on the Purification of St.
Mary the like."—Thorpe. *Ancient Laws,*
p. 367.

The following are a few excerpts from the
parish accounts :—

> 1485. *Somersetshire. Croscombe.*
> "Comys Wm. Branch and presents in
> for the font tapyr & the pascall, vjs. viijd."

> 1486. (5 Hen. VI.) *London. St. Mary
> at Hill.*
> " At Ester, for the howslyn people for
> the pascall xjs. vd."

> 1499. (14 Hen. VII.) *Reading. St.
> Lawrence.*
> Thirty-seven shillings was received for
> the Paschal.

> 1511-12. *London. St. Andrew Hubbard,
> East Cheap.*
> " *Item,* Receud At Ester for the pascall
> viijs. xjd. "

1516. "*Item*, Resseyued at Ester ffor the paskayl x^s. j^d."

1517. "*Item*, Receyued for the pascall lyght ix^s. iij^d."

1522. *Somersetshire. Croscombe.*

"The comyn in of the paschall taper vj^s. viij^d."

All the money received for the Paschal was by no means expended on it; thus, although seven shillings and eight pence was "gathered for the pascal" at St. Andrew Hubbard's in 1522-3, only three shillings and five pence "ob" appears to have been expended on the "pascal and tenebræ candell" In the previous year (1521) eight pence is only entered as received for paschal, yet four shillings and eight pence was expended on "pascal and church wax at Ester." Four years later (1525-6) fourteen shillings and three pence was received, yet two shillings and four pence only paid for Paschal.

From the churchwardens' accounts we also gather that the wax thus bought or gathered was handed over to the wax chandler (barber) to work up into the candles required, or candles were purchased direct from him :—

1447. *Thame, Oxon.*

"At Ester for the E'st' taper and the trendell x^s."

1448. "Tryndyl and Ester taper x$^{s.}$ ij$^{d.}$ ob. received."

1510. *London. St. Andrew Hubbard, East Cheap.*

"*Item*, paid for makyng of the Pascall ij$^{s.}$"

1511-12. "*Item*, paid to the wax chaunler for makyng of the pascall and the beme lighth the Judas tenebre candles and the taper halowing at the fonte vij$^{s.}$"

1517. "*Item*, paid to John burton for all manner of charges for the beme light & for the pascall xiij$^{d.}$"

"*Item*, for the paskayll makyng ij$^{d.}$"

1530-1. "*Item*, for makynge and waste off the paschall ij$^{s.}$ iv$^{d.}$"

1531-3. "Pascal old and new ij$^{s.}$ iv$^{d.}$"
The old one would appear to have been worked up with the new one.

1540. (27 Hen. VIII.) *Ludlow.*

"*Item*, payd for the holye Candylle ij$^{s.}$ vj$^{d.}$"

"*Item*, bought of M$^{r.}$ Wardene for the pascalle, a dossen li. of bolene waxe vj$^{s.}$ viij$^{d.}$"

"*Item*, payd for the makynge off the pascalle."

"*Item*, for woode and oyle to the same pascalle iiij$^{d.}$"

1541. *Ludlow.*

"*Item*, for wood to make the pascalle ij$^{d.}$" (*i.e.*, for fire to melt wax for it).

"*Item*, spende on the barber's* at the makynge of the pascalle xij$^{d.}$"

"*Item*, for oyle to the pascalle ij$^{d.}$"

1542. (33 Hen. VIII.)

"*Item*, to the barbere for the holly candelle ij$^{s.}$ vj$^{d.}$"

"*Item*, for oyle at the makyng of the pascalle."

"*Item*, the barber's breakfast at the makynge of the pascall viij$^{d.}$"

1545. "*Item*, for a sheme [seam or load] of wode at the making of the pascalle ij$^{d.}$"

"*Item*, payde for waxe to the pascalle my (John Clees) part iiij$^{s.}$ and v$^{s.}$"

Bequests were frequently made by church-folk to support and maintain the Paschal, *e.g.*, *Richard Rogers*, in 1526, left certain buildings to St. Mary Abchurch, London, for the use of the parish; half the profits to be applied to keep the house in repair, and the other half to

---

* Can the barber's pole have any connection with the Paschal? Its shape is exactly that of the Easter *Taper.*

find the Paschal within the said church for ever: any profit remaining over to be given to the poor of the parish on Good Friday yearly for ever. Merchants, yeomen and husbandmen frequently bequeathed among other things a certain number of pounds of wax for quire lights, or the Paschal taper,—twelve or twenty pounds for the latter,—above the usual funeral doles. The Winchester churchwardens' accounts show the candle to have been sometimes supported otherwise than by gift:

> 23 Hen. VII.
>> " Imprimis, at Ester, for any householder kepynge a *brode gate* shall pay to the paroche preests wages 3$^{d.}$ *item* to the Paschal ½ to St. Swithin ½."

Neither was the lavishment only of wax, much art adornment being expended on these candles, and though as a rule they were round in shape, they were at times square, as the one at Durham, which was also decorated with bright ribbons and wreathed with flowers. A MS. of the eleventh century thus shows the Paschal twined with flowers,* and an old *Ambrosian Missal* likewise mentions it:

> " Quid enim magis accommodatum, magisque festivum, quàm Jesseico flori

---

* *Rock*, t. i., p. 212.

floreis excubemus ut tedis? præsertim cum et sapientia de semetipsa cecinerit: Ego sum flos agri et lilium convallium." —*Ambro. Missal*, Ordo. Ed. Pamelio, Liturgicon, i. 346.

The author of the *Durham Rites* (p. 15) after telling us that the Paschal there lay under a "pair of faire stairs," adjoining the north door of St. Cuthbert's feretory, adds that in the time of Lent the children of the "Aumerie" were enjoined to come thither daily to dress, trim, and make it bright against the Paschal feast.

Entries also frequently appear in English mediæval churchwardens' accounts of the "garnysshyng" of candles, and especially for Corpus Christi day:

1508. *Reading. St. Lawrence.*

"*Item*, payed for xli. of grene [wax] fflowris to the forseid pasall, vj$^{d.}$"*

1511. (3 Hen. VIII.) *London. St. Margaret Pattens.*

"*Item*, iiij small Banners of lenyn clothe paynted s'vyng to hang aboute the pascall at Ester."

---

* Coats. *Hist. of Reading.*

At *York* the Great Paschal was of coloured wax and adorned, like the one at Durham, with gaily floating ribbons, and had a dove hovering over it. In some instances it was fashioned as a serpent, of which *Du Cange* (v. *Serpens*) says that it was a wooden rod made in a spiral form from which it gained its appellation "serpent," or it may have been the so-called sham or wooden candle support familiarly known as a "Judas," round which the paschal was twined —a kind of huge "triendal" of wax, long and thin, twined round a staff or ball and unwound for use in church as occasion required, very similar to the modern "bogie" or the rolls of wax tapers used at requiems in the *Oberammergau* churches.

Many of the great Paschals were painted or similarly adorned with painted flowers of wax, a custom still partially observed at *Rome* where the art of painting candles claims an origin of great antiquity. "Ast alii pictis accendant lumina ceris," says *St. Paulinus*, bishop of Nola,* and one of Raphael's most efficient and successful scholars, *Perino del Vaga*, commenced his profession in the workshop of an humble artist who gained his livelihood by painting candles for church festivals.

* *Vita S. Felicis*, p. 562.

It is very probable that they were perfumed also, as the ancients had a method of mingling perfume with the wax, which cast a continual fragrance around whilst burning, as evidenced both by *Prudentius* and *St. Paulinus* The latter writes:

> " With crowded lamps are these bright altars crown'd,
>   And waxen tapers, shedding perfume round,
>   From fragrant wicks, beam calm a scented ray," etc.

—a theory supported also by the custom prevailing out of Rome of distributing the ends of the paschal of the past year to the people to make perfume for their houses as a safeguard against evil spirits, just as little crosses made each year of the wax of the Paschal are hung on the principal doors of the Abbey of *Monte Cassino* as a protection against storm, earthquake and pestilence.   They are coloured red, and are put up with great solemnity on the feast of St. Agatha.

At *Rome* it was customary on Easter Eve for an Archdeacon to consecrate little round cakes of perfumed wax, mixed with oil and stamped with a figure of the Holy Lamb bearing the Standard of the Cross for distribution to the people in lieu of pieces of the paschal taper, which custom was the origin of those waxen images of the lamb, known as " Agnus Dei's " which the pontiffs themselves consecrated in a more august form. They were distributed on Low Sunday, the octave of Easter, to the baptized, to be burned as perfumes, symbolically in remembrance of the deliverance of man from the power of the grave at Easter by the Lamb of God.* The *Abbe Duchesne* believed the practice to be older than the Paschal Candle itself. In England, by the *Constitutions of Walter* (de Cantilupe), Bishop of Worcester (1240), after the feast of the Holy Trinity, what remained of the paschal wax was to be converted into smaller candles for the use of the altars and the poor, one authority says into tapers for the burial of the poor.

The *Venerable Bede* (734) mentions that the date of indiction and of the current year was stamped or inscribed on the Paschal Candle, or on a small plate fixed into it, a custom observed at Rome, he says, in 701 A.D.; and afterwards a long label, the original of an almanac, inscribed with a calendar of feasts was attached to it, indeed the *Council of Nicæa* required such

---

* When these were hallowed by the Pope, a post came in haste, saying, "My Lord, my Lord, these are the young lambs that have announced Alleluias; now are they come to the font." In the form of medals the custom dates from the sixth century, þut in its earlier form from the fourth century. *St. Gregory the Great* sent an Agnus Dei to the Empress Theodolinda.

a calendar to be so attached. At *Rome* they had, according to *Grancolas*,* a pillar or stat of wax on which was written with a stylus the *Breve Anni*, *i.e.*, the dates of the festivals for the ensuing year. This, however, was done at *Rome* at Christmas,† because of the new year soon to commence.‡ This somehow got mixed up with the special wax candle of Holy Saturday, but as it was not very convenient to write on a candle in France they used to write on a parchment which was then pinned to the candle. This was done (teste Grancolas) at *Rouen Cathedral*, and at *Clugny Abbey* even in the XVIIIth century. It would seem the letters A and Ω, together with inscriptions of various kinds, of which examples may be seen in *Martene* were fastened upon it.

As an almanac of feasts and other church and quire notices were anciently written on tablets of wax,—as that of the Primicier the first singer enrolled on the tablets of wax

---

* "*De l'office Ordin.*"

† *Henry III.*, on December 20th, 1247, offered in the Chapel of St. Stephen, Westminster, a large serge of pure wax 100 lbs. in weight, and painted with figures of the Blessed Virgin, the Holy Apostles, and the great Day of Doom. A similar gigantic candle was wont to be presented to St. Sebastian (on the Loire). To the boat which bore it down the river it formed a kind of mast.

‡ Bede. *De Ratione temporum*, 45.

(primus in ceris), a title dating from the ninth century;—hence arose perhaps the custom of inscribing feasts, etc., on the Paschal itself. From the following entry the custom would appear to have lingered on even in England as far as the sixteenth century:

> 1547. *Ludlow.* (Churchwardens' Accounts.)
>
> > " More to hym for makynge the allelmus upon the Paschalle opon Easter Day and paper to make them, ix^d."

The *Gemma Animæ* says the year of the Lord was to be written in the paschal taper, because Christ was the acceptable year of the Lord, whose months are the twelve apostles, whose days are the elect, and whose hours are the children baptized.*

The Ludlow Churchwardens' Accounts have the following item :

> 1555. *Ludlow.*
>
> > " Paid for ij lynkes that we helde by the pascall on Ester day in the mornynge, xx^d."

These two candles were probably symbolical of the Apostles and Prophets, as other mention is found of such being lighted from a fire of branches. (*St. John* xv. 5.)

---

* *Gemma Animæ*, de Antiq., Rit. Missæ L. iii., p. 1281.

To bless and light the Paschal with the new fire was the special prerogative of a deacon, who did so in memory of the women who brought spices and announced the tidings of the Resurrection to the Apostles.* The *Venerable Bede* says: because the disciples and not apostles buried our Lord. In the event of a priest being single-handed he put upon him the deacon's vestment—a dalmatic—for the blessing, *e.g.*, in . . . .

. . 1540, at *Westminster Abbey* . . . . .

. . a tunicle of divers colours was reserved to hallow the Pascall.

In the *Regularis Concordia*, drawn up in the reign of King Edgar for use at the benediction, we find :

> "Sabbato sancto horâ nonâ veniente abbate in ecclesiam cum fratribus, novus afferatur ignis. Posito verò cereo ante altare, ex illo accendatur ignis, quem diaconus more solito benedicens . dicat."†

By *Lanfranc's Constitutions* the rule was changed :

> "In Sabbato sancto :"— procedant ad sacrandum igneni . . . sacerdos qui

---

* 1541 (32 Hen. VIII.) *Ludlow.* "*Item,* payde to the dekens for tendynge of the pascalle, iiijd."

† *Reyner,* App., pt. iii., script. lv. 89.

ignem sacraturus est'.　　Ad altare
. . . diaconus petat ab abbate benedic-
tionem, dehinc vadat ad cereum et
benedicat eum.*

Micrologus says:

" Cereum magnum diaconus acceptâ bene-
dictione ab aliquo sacerdote debet
benedicere."†

And *Amalarius* : " quòd a diacono benedicitur
morem sequitur Romanum."‡

1541. *Ludlow.* " Payde to the dekens
for tendynge of the pascalle, iiij[d.]"

The deacon anciently blessed the candle in
the ambo, afterwards in the choir, near the
presbytery steps, *i.e.*, at the Gospel or north
side of the altar and sanctuary.

Previously to the blessing of the candle, and
during the singing of the canticle " Exultet,"
five grains of incense, representing, according
to the *IV. Council of Toledo*, the five sacred
wounds of Christ, are inserted in it. These
grains of incense are generally represented
to-day by so many pieces of gilt wood, of a
cubical form, and fastened to the candle by

---

* *Reyner*, App., pt. iii., scrip. lxxxiv. 223-4.

† *De Eccles. Observ.*, cap. 53.

‡ *De Eccles. Off.*, cap. 18, comp. *Albinus de Div. Off.*, cap. " De
Sabbato. s. Paschæ," and *Durand*, lib. vi., fo. cclxxviib.

means of a pin, a modern innovation only mentioned to be condemned. Sometimes the grains themselves are enclosed in tiny boxes of brass, and so attached to the candle by a pin. The *Auch Missal* (1491) directs the grains of incense to be fixed in the form of a star. It is this incense which is only now blessed, whereas formerly it was the candle itself. By the *Auch Missal* (1555) the deacon was directed to bless the incense during the chanting of the " Exultet," just before fixing the grains to the paschal candle. At *Rome* it was blessed by the archdeacon, in *Spain* by two deacons.

" Every Easter Eve," says the author of the " *Beehive of the Romish Churche*" (1580, f. 132), they " sing unto the wax candle which the pristes doe at that time hallow." This " singing unto the wax candle " was the ceremonial chanting of the canticle called the " Exultet," during which the grains of incense were inserted and the candle solemnly lighted. It is mentioned by *Saint Gregory*, and the form of benediction attributed to *St. Augustine* (by Martene) or *St. Ambrose*. With respect to the former the *Gallican Missal* says : " Benedictio cerac B. Augustini quam, cum ad hac diaconus esset, ed : dit et ce cinit."

This canticle is thought to be one of the few

P

if not the only extant specimen of the ancient
Ambrosian chant, whose intricacy of style,
rendering it unsuitable to the general capacity,
is generally believed to have moved St. Gregory
to arrange that system of plain chant which
bears his name, and of which the distinguishing
feature is its majestic simplicity, and is the only
style of music upon which the church has set
her seal, and adapted to her especial use.
Eunodius (d. 521), as has already been said,
preserves two forms of benediction, both
different from the " Exultet." The " Exultet "
is a peculiar composition, nearly always mis-
translated. The ceremonies (many of which
grew up around the rite in later times) were
founded on the hymn. At the words, '' incensi
hugus sacrificium," it was thought proper to
insert grains of incense; but the real meaning
is " the sacrifice of this lighted candle ! 1 "

In the *Auch Missal*, 1491, the '' Exultet " is
entitled, "Benedictio cerei quam zozimus papa
constituit," and in it are some verbal differences,
additions, and omissions. In the *Cathedral* of
Pisa was preserved, and may be still is, a
relique of the early part of the twelfth century,
consisting of a parchment containing the
" Exultet," as usually sung upon Sabbato
Santo. Figures in miniature, plants and

animals may be seen here and there painted upon it.* These "Exultet" rolls are among some of the earliest liturgical codices, and are much illuminated, and being narrow stretch out at a great length.† One at *Monte Cassino* is twelve feet long, and a little more than nine inches broad.‡ As the deacon unwound it, it fell outside the ambo. *Dr. Rock* (t. i., p. 212) shows a deacon in the ambo singing the "Exultet."

After its blessing the Paschal was lighted with the new fire (see Rock, i., 212) by the triple candle—a three-fold candle rising from one stock, or of three candles plaited together and divided above, in signification of the mystery of the Blessed Trinity, three Persons in One God, or the light of the Triune God shining to the world through Christ. Sometimes this candle took the form of a serpent, and, twined about a staff or lance, headed the processions in lieu of the cross on this day. It burned only during the office of Holy

---

* See *Archæological Journal,* vol. 34, p. 321, a paper by Mr. E. M. Thompson, "On an Exultet of the twelfth century," with illustrations showing the blessing, lighting, and censing of the candle.

† Generally speaking they are about 11 inches wide, and over 22 feet long. The specimen in the British Museum, No. Ad. 30,337, has 14 distinct pictures.

‡ Desciibed by Caravita, *I codici e le Arte a Monte-Cassino,* i , p. 304.

Saturday morning, after which it was taken away and used no more. *Le Tableau de la Croix represénté dans les cérémonies de la Sainté Messe;* printed by François Mazot, 1653, has an illustration of a boy, habited as an angel with wings, engaged in the act of lighting the Paschal candle with a wax serpent thus twined about a rod.*

The Serpent (or the Paschal, itself a type of the pillar of fire which went before Israel in the wilderness†) was carried before the candidates for baptism in the procession to the font on this day, where new believers were to pass through the waters of baptism, as Israel through the Egyptian bondage through the Red Sea (which prefigured Baptism, thus to excite a recollection of the illumination of the Holy Spirit whilst they are going to the Church), in order to arrive at the real promised land, a state of grace indicated by that heavenly column of the gospel light of Christ shining on them day and night, as the fiery column did the Israelites of old.

---

* The *Transactions of St. Paul's Ecclesiological Society,* vol. II., p. 126, fig. 9, gives a print of it.

† The Paschal has the same symbolical interpretation when it precedes the Pope, as, according to the *Ordo Romanus,* it should do during the whole Paschal week.

According to the *Auch Missal* (1491), the serpent was borne on days other than Easter Eve, for it directs that after None (Maundy Thursday and Good Friday) the bishop and ministers, previously to the Adoration of the Cross, approached the altar with a sculptured figure of a serpent twined round a rod, and lights. The 1555 edition of the same Missal says that at the new fire blessing the deacon carried a staff, about which was entwined the figure of a serpent, holding in its mouth an unlighted candle. At *Fossombrone, Osino,* was observed a special procession on Easter Day, in which the Paschal Candle was borne to the baptistery, where a hymn was sung in honour of the mystery of the Resurrection and Sacrament of Propitiation, and after reciting the antiphon, "Regina Cœli," the procession returned to the quire.

As the Paschals were frequently of great size and weight it became common to support them by constructing the lower part standing upon the pricket of the candlestick of wood painted to look like wax and possibly at times even coated with it, upon which the real candle was set. Sometimes these stocks were made entirely of wax, at others they consisted of a case, the end of which only was closed with wax sufficient for the purpose. These false candles usually went by the name of JUDASES, and doubtless were so called after the traitor. The general supposition is that they were exclusively connected with the support of the great Paschal, which is by no means the case, as' the parish accounts and church inventories abundantly prove:

> 1455. (33 Hen. VI.) *Bristol. St. Ewen* (destroyed).
>
> "*Item,* one Judas of the pascal, 12 judas for the 12 square tabres [tapers or torches] be for the rood a boue."
>
> 1466. *London. St. Stephen, Coleman Street.*
>
> "*Item,* j Judas to sett Candell ther on w^t a fote pteynyg therto."
>
> 1476. *London. The Smiths Company.*
>
> "A new holle to Judas."
>
> 1487. "iiij new torchis and painting of Judasses."
>
> 1516. "iiij new Judasses" (the weight varying from 26-30 lbs.).
>
> 1481. *London. The Carpenters Company.*
>
> "*Item,* payd for stuff of ye Judass^s ij^d."
>
> "*Item,* payd for iiij platys, xj^d."
>
> 1482. "Expens' for Torchis, 30 lb. **wax,** p. li. v^d ob. xiii^s ix^d."

"*Item*, j doss.' Reseu, xxj^d·, payd for the makyng; iij^s· iv^d·"

1485. *London. The Coopers Company.*

"Payed for tember and the makyng of iiij Judassus for the torchis, xiv^d·"

"*Item*, p'd ffor platus to ye Judassus off Iron, vij^d· and bolts."

"*Item*, p'd for iiij new torchis that weyyeth xxvj^lb· at iij^d· li., vi^s· viij^d·"

1500. *Bristol. St. Ewen* (destroyed).

"Ten new Jadases and ten bolls to hold them."

1524. *London. St. Margaret, Westminster.*

"Paid for twelve Judacis to stand with the tapers, ij^s·"

1559. *London. St. Christopher-le-Stock.*

"*Item*, ther beth vj Judas staves for Torches peynted havyng iche a Castele gilded to sett Inne Torchets to bere with the Sacrement on Corpus Cristy daye & other tymes."

From its connection with the Judas, the Paschal Candle may have gained its name of the "Jewes Light" or the "Judas Light"

---

* The term Judas is frequently used in the plural in the Inventories, thus in Peacock's *Lincolnshire Church Furniture*, "albes, paxes, Iudaces with suche trifelinge tromperey," "clappers Iudaces and a sepulker" were destroyed in the 1st year of Eliz. at Epworth in the Isle of Axholme and Skellington respectively.

just as its candlestick was known as the " Judas Candlestick."*   The Herse for the Tenebræ Lights was also called in some places the " Judas Tree " or Judas Cross, perhaps from being made of elder wood, which played a frequent part in these Holy Week ceremonies, Judas being said to have hanged himself on such a tree.†   So the inventories:

> 1566.   Ap. 30.   *Wintertonne.*
>
> " *Item*, the Iewes light, the pascall post, the sepulchre, the maydens light " (burned 2nd Eliz.).‡
>
> 1566.   March 29.   *Newtonne.*
>
> " *Item*, . . . one Judas Candlestick " sold and broken.
>
> 1552.   *Thame, Oxon.*
>
> " *Item*, for l$^{li.}$ of syxes for the Judas light, xj$^{d.}$"
>
> 1473-98.   *Accounts of Lord High Treasurer of Scotland.*
>
> " *Item*, for the mending of the sepulture, ... and Judas crois, iij$^{s.}$"§

---

* Probably in the generality of cases the Tenebre Candles and Herse is meant. "The Iewes Light and the Pascall Post" are both mentioned in the Inventory of Wintertonne, Lincoln, 1566.

† See Sir J. Mandeville " *Voiage and Travail*," &c., p. 112, ed. 1725; Pulci *Morgante* Mag. C. xxv. st. 77; Gerarde, *Herbal*, p. 1428, ed. 1663.

‡ Peacock. *Lincolnshire Church Furniture.*

§ " *Expens maid aponne the Kingis Chapell.*" A.D. 1494-5.

1557. *Ludlow.*

"*Item*, for nayles for the Judas crosse, j^d"

"*Item*, for a piece of tymber and mendynge the same, ij^{d.}"

Some think that the Easter taper gained its name of "Judas Candle" from the small wax figures of Judas which were sometimes hung upon it. As the candlestick was frequently one of seven branches, the Judas would be placed upon the seventh or upright branch in the middle, and thus with the great paschal rising above it would come into somewhat close proximity to the vaulting. *Durandus** says that "in some churches the candles are put out with a wax hand, which signifies the hand of Judas, which was, as it were of wax,—that is, flexible to evil, by which Christ our King and true light was betrayed, and as much as in Him lay, extinguished."†

The Accounts of *St. Mary-at-Hill, London,* for 1511, have a memorandum which explains

---

* *Rat. Div. Off.*, lib. vi. cap. lxxii. 24. · "In quibusdam quoque ecclesiis candelæ quadam *manu cerea* extinguuunter, quæ significat manum *Judæ* : de qua Dominus dixit : Qui intingit manum mecum, etc. Quæ fuit quasi cerea, id est, ad malum flexibilis per quam Christus Rex noster et vera lucerna traditus fuit, et quantum in illo fuit extinctus."

† Stopford's translation. *Pagano. Papismus,* or Parallel between Rome Pagan and Rome Christian, 1675, p. 166.

exactly the position and make of the Judas in its connection with the Paschal : "the judas of the pastal, *i.e.*, the tymbre that the wax of the pastel is driven upon, weigeth 7 lbs." Other parish accounts support this :

1493-4. (8 & 9 Hen. VII.)——— *(Churchwardens' Accounts).

"*Item*, paid to Willm Bruer peynt' for peyntyng the Judasis of the Paschall and of the Rode lofte, xx^{d.}"

"*Item*, paid the xx day of Aprill to Thomas Arlome Joynour for stuff and workmanship planyng and settyng vp the said Judasis of the paschall & of the Rode lofte . . . iij^{s.} vj^{d.}"

19-21 Hen. VII. "*Item*, paid A Carpent' for iij new Judasys on the Rood loft & naylis to the same, v^{d.}"—and so several other items, and churchwardens closing their account for the year 1525-6 observe —"so we have lefte to the cherch xiij torches good and bade also v ends of torches for Judasses."

The use of these torch-ends is explained by a further entry :

1533-4. "*Item*, paid for mendyng the Judac' that the torches stode in, & for an Iron pyne made to sett in an olde torche & for waxe to closse the torche & the end togeder w^t his labour, xxij$^{d.}$"

Mediæval church accounts have frequent reference to the Judas Candle and its making ; the following are a few samples

5 Hen. VI. *London. St. Mary-at-Hill.* "For a pece of timber to the new Pascall."

1431. *London. St. Peter Cheap.* "*Item*, j judas for to hold torches ends in."

1555. "*Item*, payd for a Judas Candell weyinge ij$^{lli.}$ ij$^{d.}$"

1465-6. *London. St. Andrew Hubbard, East Cheap.* "A pound Candell for Judas."

1466-8. "*Item*, for makyng of Judas Candell, j$^{d.}$"

1476-8. "1 lb. quarteron for Judas Candle."

1480-2. "Paid for a candill case, iij$^{d.}$"*

1490-1. "Dressing ten torches and one Judas."

---

* 1466-8. *St. Andrew Hubbard, East Cheap.* "*Item*, for wyre to the paskall, iiijd." ? to keep Paschal in its place.

1510-12. "*Item*, paid for a pound of Candelas in wax for tenebre lighth upon the Judas, viij$^{d.}$"

1511-12. "*Item*, paid to the wax chaunler for makyng of 'the Judas.'"

1525, etc. "Paid for Judas Candylles, viij$^{d.}$"

1527-8. "Paid for tenebre Candelles and Judas Candelles, ij$^{d.}$"

1531-3. "Two Judas Candles, xij$^{d.}$"

1540. "*Item*, paid to the waxe chandeler for the toppys of the torches, vij$^{s.}$ ix$^{d.}$"

1540. *Oxford.* *St. Giles* (MS. Inventory) "for a pound of belas (wood) for Judas light."

14 Hen. VII. *Reading.* *St. Lawrence.* "*Item*, payed for makyng leng' [longer] Mr. Smyth's molde w^t a Judas for the Pascall, vj$^{d.}$"

1505. "*Item*, payd for xxviij$^{li.}$ wex for a stoke to the pascal & to the font tapyr and for to rem the rod light p' o le li. v$^{d.}$ sm^a xj$^{s.}$ viij$^{d.}$"*

1523. "*Item*, payd for payntyng the lent awl'cloth and the Judas, xij$^{d.}$"

1519. *Reading.* *St. Giles.* "Paid for making a Judas for the pascall, iiij$^{d.}$"

---

* This would show the "Judas" was sometimes entirely of wax.

1524. *London. St. Margaret, Westminster.*

" 1¾ lb. [paschal], the Judas taper, 1 lb."

1552. *Thame, Oxon.*

" iij^{d.} for making the Judas and y^e sepu'lere."

" *Item*, for ij^{li.} of sixes for y^e Judus light, xxij^{d.}"

6 Edward VI. *Kent. Lee.*

" *Item*, a case to put torches or tapers in."

1554. *Ludlow.*

" *Item*, paid for tymber for the pascalle, vj^d "

" *Item*, for pentynge of the post to the said pascalle, vj^{d.}"

1555-6. " Paid for mendynge the pascalle stocke, iij^{d.}"

1533. " *Item*, paid for payntyng of the Judas or stock of the Rood lyght."

After its lighting the great Paschal is placed upon its candlestick—the Paschal Post or Column—a tall single standard candlestick shaped sometimes as a column, and at others as a large seven-branched candelabrum. It was constructed of a variety of material—wood, latten, iron, or of the precious metals and marbles, often of fine workmanship, elaborately wrought and exquisitely adorned with sculpture, bronze, or curiously tesselated in rich and elegant mosaic. Sometimes it consisted of a twisted or ornamented shaft of verde antique, with a Corinthian base and a capital wrought either in gilt, bronze, or white marble, of which the early basilican churches of Rome contain some notable examples upon the left side of the ambons, as at *St. Maria* in *Cosmedin, St. Agnes, St. Clement,* and one of the twelfth century of colossal size at *St. Peter's Without.** One stands on the north side of the altar at *St. Anthony's, Padua,* and another in the atrium of *Capua Cathedral,* where three other lights in honour of the Holy Trinity are kindled on a staff or paschal post below it.† Out of Rome the constructional Easter candlestick did not obtain, its place being supplied by the great

---

* Being of marble encrusted with mosaic, these massive structures are really monumental, and *on suite* with the *cancelli* and *ambones* of the choir. It seems though generally these candlesticks were not always attached to the ambons, as witness the example figured in Plate CLXXXXIV., *Rome Bibliotheque de la Minerve*—11th century—where an iron candlestick stands upon the ground. Some think them "Gospel" candlesticks.

† Such as the superb seven-branched candle-tress given by King Canate to Winchester in 1035, and by Prior Conrad to Canterbury in 1108, or that crowning the shrine of St. Etheldreda at Ely. Probab'y many of these and the "Jesses" were utilized for the Paschal.

lofty candelabrum of brass or latten, either with or without the seven additional branches.*

The author of the *Durham Rites* (p. 9) has given us a description of the magnificent candlestick which supported the great Paschal there in its hey-day. It stood upon a four-square sixteen plank of wood, against the first grees or step, hard behind the three basins of silver that hung before the high altar; at every corner of the plank an iron ring, which the feet of the paschal adjoined, representing four flying dragons, as also four evangelists with six fine candlesticks for tapers to stand in above the dragons; in four quarters four crystal stones, and in four small dragons' four heads four crystal stones. On every side of the four dragons curious antique work, as beasts and men upon horseback, with bucklers, bows and shafts and knots, with broad leaves spread upon the knots. Six candle flowers of metal, three on every side, in each a taper of wax and in

---

* In France the Candlestick stood in the Rood Loft (at Paris and St. Denis on the top of the Sanctuary Steps). Malcolm "*London Rediv.*" (vol. ii., p. 66), says the church of All Hallows, London Wall, contained a rood loft and a representation of Judas in it, which was painted in 1455 for "xiijd." Some say it is absurd to suppose that wooden candlesticks were made in the shape of the traitor; yet candlesticks and torch-holders of the period were frequently made in human shape. See "Shakespeare." Boswell, V. xvi., p. 410. Notes. Romeo says: "I'll be a candle-holder and look on."

the top principal flower the Paschal, "that in latitude did contain almost the bredth of the quire, in longitude that did extend to the height of the vault," wherein did stand a long piece of wood, reaching within a man's length to the uppermost vault of the church, and whereon stood a great long taper of square wax. The whole being of latten metal it glistened as gold, and was estimated one of the rarest monuments in England. It is said to be now in the possession of some foreign cathedral.

At Westminster Abbey, at the time of the Dissolution, was " A Crosse for the Holy Candyll with a pryk for a taper in the mydds." It was of silver and gilt, with arms of crossed keys and of the monastery, enamelled in the four ends of the crosses.

Few, if any, of these grand old Paschal candlesticks have been left to us. The *Museum* at *South Kensington* preserves the one from *Gloucester Cathedral.* It is a pricket candlestick of white metal gilt, of about 1110-15 A.D., inscribed, " Abbatis Petri Gregis et devotio mites me dedit ecclesie sancti Petri Gloecestre," and is a wonderful example of elaborate art. To see the Paschal Candlestick in its old perfection of beauty we must go to *Belgium* and the *Low Countries.* At *St. Leonard, Léan*

(Province of Brabant, Belgium), is such an one. Of "laiton," it rises to upwards of $18\frac{1}{2}$ feet high, its hexagonal base resting upon the backs of three lions and three hounds. From this base rises a species of tree (vine), divided in three massive stems. At a height of three and a half feet is fixed an open-worked brass book desk, above which stands an elegant statue of St. Leonard the patron, upon a moulded corbel, with a candle bracket in front. Above the statue the vine stem divides into six branches, bearing clusters of grapes and leaves, from the midst of which starts up the central stem, the "tree" of the cross bearing the figure of the Crucified Saviour   The six lower branches support candle basins and sconces, whilst the three smaller ones, upheld by flying arches, sustain statues of the Blessed Virgin, SS. John and Mary Magdalene. The central stem continuing upwards terminates in a large basin and pricket, upon which the great Paschal is fixed. This pillar of wax, of nearly ten feet high and seven inches in diameter, is richly adorned with exquisite paintings, representing the Resurrection and Ascension of our Lord, by a great artist. Rising to a total height of nearly thirty feet, its lighting was accomplished from the triforium, as at Coutances and Durham, and a splendid sight must this veritable " tree of light " have presented when its great " master candle " was lighted and the small multitude of the lesser branches added their brilliancy to the scene.

Other remarkable Paschal Candlesticks exist in use at the Premonstrant *Abbey of Postel*, near Turnhout (Campine) ; at *Parc Abbey*, near Louvain (both of 12th century) ; at *St. Mary, Tongres ; St. Trond ; St. Vaast*, of Gaurain, near Tournai (3 branches) ; and at *St. Ghislain*, where the central sconce, when not holding the Paschal, is occupied by a statue of St. Catherine, in brass. It was given to the church in 1442, and has a prayer for the souls of the donors and the name of its maker inscribed upon it.

The old English name for this candlestick was the Paschal Post,* from which may be concluded that its construction was often of wood. The *Statutes* of 1250 ; of *John* (Peckham), Archbishop of Canterbury, 1280 ; the *Synod of Exeter*, 1287 ; the *Constitutions of Robert* (de Winchelsey), Archbishop of Canterbury, 1305 ; of *Simon*, Archbishop of Canterbury, 1368 ; and the *Visitation Articles* of Bishop Bonner,

---

* Rock. *Church of our Fathers*, vol. i., p. 212, gives an engraving of a paschal post and candle. Two " pascall postes " out of *Paunton Parva* Church, Lincoln, were sold and burnt in 1564.

each require the parishioners to provide (*inter alia*) "a candlestick for the Paschal tapers," which word "candlestick" must be construed, if the church accounts and inventories are to be taken into account, to mean a hanging basin, such as is the custom to-day in the diocese of *Milan, e.g. :—*

> 5 Hen. VI. *London.* *St. Mary-at-Hill.*
> "Payd for a dysh of pewter for the Paskall."
>
> 1454-6. *London.* *St. Andrew Hubbard.*
> "*Item*, Recued for a dyssh of laten for the Paschall, iv$^{s.}$"
> "*Item*, Recued for a Rope for a Paskall."
>
> 1466. *London.* *St. Stephen, Coleman Street.*
> "ij disshes for the pascalle w^t Cordes that ptainis ther to."
> "*Item*, ij boltys of Iron hangyng on the Corde of the Pascalle and hy in the chaunsell Rofe."
>
> 1542 (34 Hen. VIII.).
> "A lamp for the pascall."
>
> 1470 (10 Ed. IV.). *London.* *St. Margaret Pattens.*
> "*Item*, a bason of peaut'r w^t iiij small bollys for the Pascall."

1498. *Reading. St. Lawrence.*

" *Item*, payed for the Paschal bason and the hangyng of the same, xviijs. "

" *Item*, payed for vij pendaunts for ye same basin and the caryage fro London, iijs. "

1513. " *Item*, payd for makyng clene of the basyn for the pascall ayenst Est."

1518. *London. St. Peter Cheap.*

" A chayne of latten that dyd hange the Paskall."

" *Item*, the Paskall with cheynys and other necessaries."

1555. " *Item*, payd for a pascall bason."

" *Item*, payd for a Rope to hang the paskall bason by, xijd. "

1520-1. *London. St. Andrew Hubbard, East Cheap.*

" *Item*, paid for a Cord for the pascall, ijd. "

1541. *Ludlow.*

" *Item*, for mendynge of the pascalle borde, iiijd. "

1547. " *Item*, for iiij clammes [iron clamps] for the pascalle bordes, ijd. "

1554. " *Item*, for pentynge of the post to the pascalle, vjd. "

1542. (34 Hen. VIII.) *Westminster. St. Stephen.*

"ij latten deskys with a stonderd for the Pascall of latten."

"j stykke of sylver parcell gylt for the Holy Candell, viij oz."

1542. *London. St. Magnus.*

"iiij pillors of latten for the paskall."

2 Ed. VI. *Westminster. St. Margaret.*

"*Item*, a Pascall Basyn and a Lamp of latten."

1552. (6 Ed. VI.) *Camberwell Parish Church* (St. Giles).

"*Item*, ix boules & one for the paxall."

1552. *Worcester Black Friars.*

"*Item*, a lamp with another y^t holde ye Pascall."

1552. *London. St. Nicholas, Cole Abbey.*

"Piece of latten for the Pascall."

Herts. Pelham ffurneaux.

"A Paschal candlestick."

1552. *Kent. Hynxhell.*

"*Item*, a gret candelstycke of yron for the paschall."

1552. *Kent. Bromley.*

"Lamp of latten for the Pascal."

1552. *Canterbury. All Saints.*

"A standard for the pascalle."

1552. *Surrey. Thursley, St. Michael.*
" *Item*, a bason for a lampe."

1552. *Surrey. Wonersh, St. Leonard.*
" *Item*, j paskall bason brokyn."

1552. *Surrey. Newington, St. Mary.*
" *Item*, a table on iron candlestick."
" *Item*, x pascall staves."

1552. *Cheam. St. Dunstan.*
" *Item*, a pascall candlestick of latten."

1557. *London. St. Michael, Cornhill.*
" Paid for mendynge the fote of the Paskall & hange the Roode lofte at Easter, vj^{d}."

1557. *Bristol. Christ Church.*
" *Item*, for a cord to hange ye pascall."

1529. *London St. Christopher-le-Stock.*
" *Item*, ther is a lampe hanging before the Rode in a basyn of laton and a basyn with Cheynes and a Sterre of laton for to hange Inne the Pascall at the Season of Esterne "

The sparse mention of the Paschal Candlestick in the inventories of minor churches would lead to the belief that it was not in all. Upon the altar steps of *Canterbury Cathedral* may be seen the socket for the paschal post, and in the pavement of the presbytery steps of

St. David's Cathedral, on the north side, is a mortice conjectured for a similar purpose. At *Southwell* it still stands near the altar.

Pope Innocent III. mentions a curious ritual use of this Paschal column, besides the up-holding of the Paschal ·

> " In quibusdam basilicis circa medium chori, manipulus stuppæ super columnam appenditur, cui pontifex ignem apponit, ut in conspectu populi subito combu-rantur."—*De Sacro Altaris Mysterio*, lib. ii., cap. ix.

The tow is now burnt at the coronation of a newly chosen pontiff, not on the column, but from the top of a long silver staff, being set on fire by the Master of the Ceremonies.

The Paschal Candle burns continually throughout Easter week, at mattins, mass, and evensong; on all Sundays till the Ascension, on the Feasts of St. Mark, SS. Philip and James, at mass only; on Lady Day and the Invention of the Cross as during Easter week. On the morrow of the Ascension it is taken away in the morning. At *Rome* it was put out at the words "Assumptus est," in the Ascension Day Gospel; the *Cordeliers* removed it at None at the antiphon, " I ascend to my Father"; at *Soissons* it burnt for four consecutive days*; at *Albi* it was not removed till the benediction of the font in the Vigil of Pentecost,† and in some places it remained till *after* Pentecost—the flame being extinguished in holy water by means of a sponge, or by a (Judas) hand of wax.

I can find no entry as to its removal in the accounts of churchwardens, etc., but the following in reference to the Sepulchre Light will serve :—

> 1514. *Bristol. St. Ewen* (destroyed).
> " *Item*, ffor marchynge off the sepulchre light, viij^d."

The Paschal Candle is full of symbolic meaning. *Unlighted* it was figurative of Christ's death and repose in the tomb, and when *lighted* it was a type of the splendour and glory of His Resurrection. In the wick is seen an emblem of the human Spirit of Christ; in the wax the pure product of " cleanly bees," a type of His Body, formed in the pure womb of Blessed Mary; in the halo of the great flame is shewn His Divinity. The lighting of it exhibits the grace and doctrine which Christ came on earth to diffuse. The new fire, struck from a flint, represents the " rock which was Christ "; the

---

* Martene, *de Ant. Eccles. Rit.*, lib. iv., c. 24.
† *Ordinance* of Louis d'Amboise, July 5, 1476.

fire produced, the Holy Ghost, just as the taper prefigured our Lord and expressed the column of fire preceding Israel in their wanderings; and the new fire kindled, the Gospel—the new doctrine of Christ. The five grains of incense inserted are in memory of the Five Wounds of our Lord, as also of the spices (a mixture of myrrh and aloes) in which His Body was embalmed. All the tapers, previously extinguished, are lighted from the new fire, because our Lord, standing in the midst of His Disciples, and shewing them His Hands and His Side, breathed on them, and said, " Receive ye the Holy Ghost." According to the *Venerable Bede*, the seven-branched candelabrum itself is " the type of the Seven Gifts of the Holy Ghost, of the Seven Churches, and of Christ Himself"; and to St. Gregory, who says ·

" Christ became the Candelabrum of the World."*

NOTE.—I was anxious to identify the Paschal with the Sepulchre Light, and, although those

---

* *Sir Thomas More* speaks of the hallowing of fire, the fount, and the *Paschal Lamb.* *Walafrid Strabo* condemns the practice of placing near or under the altar on Good Friday, lamb's flesh, which received benediction and was eaten on Easter Day ; to which custom the Greeks alluded, in the 9th century, when they accused the Latins of offering (presenting) a lamb on the altar, with a symbolical meaning. In ancient times the Pope and Cardinals ate lamb on Easter Day.

learned in the matter say it cannot be done, yet there is much to lead to a supposition that in later times it may have had some connection, as the following excerpt from the Parish Accounts may prove :

1555. *St. Michael's, Cornhill.*

"Paide for the Joyenour for makinge the Sepullere the Pashal and the Tene-bars to the same."

Another account speaks of

"j candylstycke of yrne afore yᵉ sepul-chre."

And the "marchynge off the sepulchre lyght" could be none other than the distinct cere-monial act connected with the Paschal Candle itself.

Easter Eve.

AFTER the blessing of the Paschal, the reading of the Lessons, and the seven-fold and the five-fold Litanies, the blessing of the Font takes place. The septiform or seven-fold Litany was chanted by seven boys in surplices, or sometimes by seven subdeacons. The five-fold Litany, sung by five Deacons in surplices, is begun in the midst of the quire, and continued on the way to the font. The Sarum *Processionale* orders that the Litany, after the blessing of the font on Easter Eve, be sung by three clerks *superior gradi*, vested in silk copes, two red, the third white.

By the *Councils of Ireland* (456), *Gerona* (517), and several English Synods of the 11th and 13th centuries, baptism was only administered on the Eves of Easter and Pentecost, except in cases of necessity.

In later times the Font, like the water at the Epiphany by the Greeks, was solemnly hallowed,

the water being expressly consecrated in remembrance of the Easter baptism. In the 4th
century in the East, the Greek Church observed
the custom of baptizing catechumens, and consecrating water in the font on this Eve. At
Rome they still keep up the ancient custom
of baptizing Jews at this time. The reading of
the twelve Exercises or Lections (the ancient
Prophecies) was primarily intended for the
instruction of the catechumens baptized on this
night. Four Prophecies were read on the
Pentecost Vigil at Auch (Missal 1491). *St.
Ambrose* alludes to the custom of washing the
feet of the newly-baptized in imitation of Christ's
washing of the disciples' feet.

In the parish accounts of *St. Mary Hill,
London*, for 1520 and other years appears the
extraordinary and frequent charge: "For
water to be hallowed on Maundy Thursday and
Easter Even for the fountains, ij[d.]" This
hallowed water was carried away by the people
at the Reformation period, in the same way
as the faithful of the Greek Church took the
water home after the mass on the Feast of the
Epiphany, a custom alluded to by *St. John
Chrysostom.*

Anciently the newly-blessed Paschal Candle
headed the procession of neophytes to the

waters of salvation (Holy Baptism), as the pillar of fire led the children of Israel to the saving waters of the Red Sea. The *Sarum Missal* does not explicitly say the Paschal Candle is so borne, but the " Candle for the blessing of the Font." This "font candle" or " light about the font "* was generally a candle of a pound weight, and is frequently mentioned in the Accounts, *e.g. :*

> 1510-12. *St. Andrew Hubbard, East Cheap.*
>
> " *Item*, paid for A pound taper for hallowing at fonte and the cros candelas, viij^{d.}"

This taper, or it may be the Paschal, was borne in the procession in a cloth or towel :

> 1550. *St. Dunstan in the East, London.* (MS. Inventory.)
>
> " *Item*, a fyne towell wrought w^t nedle worke for the Taper on Easter evyn."
>
> 1552. (6 Ed. 6.) *St. Elphege, Canterbury.*
> " *Item*, a towell for the fonte taper."

Around the font was also wrapped a cloth at its hallowing on Easter and Whitsun Eves :

> 1455. *St. Ewen, Bristol.*
> " *Item*, a White Cloth for the Font."

---

* 1466-8. *St. Andrew Hubbard, East Cheap.*

The chrysmatory, which was also borne in the procession, was likewise enveloped in a cloth or towel:

1450. *St. Ewen, Bristol.*

"*Item,* one towell of Rede sylke with other coluers to bere the chrysmatory; with two long cottens one of them whyt with the frenge Red and the other dyed Red Coloyr."

London   St. Michael le Querne. (MS. Inventory.)

" ij towells of sendall to beare the crysmatory yn."

At *St. Mary, Woolnorth,* was a Sudary cloth of Turkey silke for the same purpose. In 1498 at *St. Lawrence, Reading,* it was of ray silke; at *St. Dunstan in the East* (4 Edward VI.), "a cloth of Turkey worke."*

After the blessing, the water in the Font is divided in the form of a cross, and some of it is scattered to the four quarters of the world. Wax from the candle is dropped into the font in the form of a cross, and the candle itself is dipped into it (in some places a triple immersion

---

* At *Westminster Abbey,* in 1540, the "Skons berar" wore a tunicle of red satin on Easter Even; there were also two others of divers colours, one to hallow the Paschal, the other for him that beareth the Dragon.

of the candle took place). Then the people are sprinkled with this Easter water. Formerly catechumens were baptized and confirmed at this portion of the ceremonial, but now oil and Chrism are *not* poured into the font unless there is anyone to be baptized. On the return to the altar the chanter cried aloud *Accendite* (Light) and all the candles were instantly lighted, the *Gloria in Excelsis* sung, and all the bells rang joyously.*

At the Reformation the parishioners marched seven times round the font in procession at *Salisbury*, on every day in Easter week; a procession was made with four rulers of the quire to incense the font. At *Chartres*, during Easter week, all the capitular clergy go to the font, with the subchanter preceding the junior canons, carrying white wands, in allusion to the white robes of the baptized.

Easter Week was called the Neophyte's Octave, and during every day the competents came in their white robes, and with lights in their hands, until the Sunday in Albes (Neophyte's Day, Octave of Infants,—Low Sunday), the eve of which (the Sabbath in Albes) was called the close of Easter, a custom

---

* There is no such *Accendite* in the Sarum books.

which lasted from the time of Tertullian till after the date of Gratian. Low Sunday was called the Sunday in Albes from the white dresses worn by the newly baptized. On this day, or the 4th Sunday after Easter, the commemoration of the last Easter baptism was called the Annotine Easter.

The celebration of the Vigil of Easter is mentioned by Tertullian, the Apostolical Canons, Eusebius, Lactantius, St. Gregory of Nazianzen, Jerome, and Chrysostom. On the testimony of Eusebius, and the two Gregories (of Nazianzen, and Nyssa), we learn that the churches and streets were lighted so brilliantly that the night seemed transformed into day, in honour of the illumination of the grave by the Resurrection of the Light of Life and of the World from the dead. St. Gregory Nazianzen calls it the " holy night of illuminations." It was also called the Sabbath of Lights. King Ethelwulf (857) by will left 200 mancas of gold to be divided between the churches of SS. Peter and Paul at Rome to provide lights on Easter Eve.*

In the old days the services continued in the

---

* Asser, *Annales Rerum Gestarum, Ælfredi,* etc., p. 472.

churches until past midnight to welcome in the dawn. The Holy Eucharist was celebrated after Vespers on the Eve, in anticipation of Easter, as it was later by an *Irish Council* (456), and the *Sarum Use*, when the Gloria in Excelsis formed the Introit, and bells rang out joyously for the dawn of Easter. At *Milan* the deacon announced thrice in the mass, " Christ our Lord is risen," the choir thundering back the words, " Deo Gratias."

Before Mattins and bell ringing, the clerks meet in the Church and light all the candles throughout it, and the Host is taken from the Sepulchre with candle-bearers and thurifers, and placed again in the Pyx hanging over the altar; afterwards the Cross is likewise taken from the Sepulchre and carried to an altar (at *Sarum* in the northern part of the Church). The bells are rung with a clash, the Antiphon sung, and the Collect said, and all genuflect with joy, and at once venerate the Cross, which done, all the crosses and images throughout the Church are uncovered, and the bells rung for Mattins in the usual way.

.   .   .   .   .

In *England,* from Easter Day to Ascension, a processional cross of crystal or beral was used. There was such a one at *Durham*, *Winchester* and other places, *e.g.*:

> 1431. *St. Peter Cheap, London.*
> "*Item*, j crosse of birell garnesshede wᵗ silver."
> 1526. "*Item*, for mendyng of the great berall crosse hed that was broken."
> *Westminster Abbey.* (Dissolution.)
> "iij sides of a broken crosse of birralle."
> "a crosse of chalcedony."

At *Maestricht* is preserved a twelfth century cross of rock crystal, which in the sunlight flashes up and shines like fire. On Easter Day at *Orleans* two processional crosses were carried at Mass and Vespers.

Laus Deo.

Index.

Catholic

Theological Books,

PUBLISHED BY

THOMAS BAKER,

72, NEWMAN STREET, 72

LONDON,

W.

N.B.—All the publications contained in this Catalogue are issued at net prices, and under no circumstances can any discount be given to the public. The books may be obtained either directly from the Publisher, or through any local Bookseller.

JOHN RUYSBROEK.

REFLECTIONS FROM THE MIRROR OF A MYSTIC,

Being Gleanings from the Works of
JOHN RUYSBROEK

("Doctor Ecstaticus") a Mystic of the XIVth Century.

Translated by EARLE BAILLIE.

Cr. 8vo, cloth extra - - - - - - **2s. net.**

Dionysius Carthusianus, speaking of Ruysbroek, says : "His authority I believe to be that of a man to whom the Holy Ghost has revealed His secrets."

"Ce moine possédait un des plus sages, des plus exacts, et des plus subtils organes philosophiques qui ai jamais existé."—*Maeterlinck.*

"The 'Reflections' contain sixteen chapters of the choicest thoughts of the great Mystic. . . . We have great pleasure in recommending this work, which will well repay the reader."—*The Tablet, May*, 1905.

"Ruysbroek, from whose spiritual writings this excellent work has been compiled by Ernest Hello, was born in Belgium in the year 1203. They contain lessons of piety for persons in every state of life, and will help the sincere reader on the road to perfection. . . . We have great pleasure in recommending this work."—*Tablet.*

"It is good for modern busy people to read such selections, they will serve as a sedative for feverish states and over-active propensities, shedding calm without inducing inaction."—*Catholic Examiner, Bombay.*

"A welcome contribution to the ascetic literature of our language."—*Ave Maria.*

"The one criticism that we pass upon it is that it is so short. . . . Every book of selections from the old mystics is a favour to be cordially appreciated : for the old masters of prayer are incomparably the best."—*New York Catholic World.*

XXV. PLAIN CATHOLIC SERMONS,

With a Synopsis of each Sermon,

BY

Fr. CLEMENT HOLLAND.

Second Series.

Thick crown 8vo, cloth - **4s. 6d. net.**

CONTENTS :—Sufferings of the Poor at Christmas—Christ and the Youth of To-Day—The True Bread of Eternal Life—Indifferentism in Religion God and His Creatures—The Man Degraded beneath the Brute—The Privileges of Mary—Pope and King—Ambassadors of Christ—Do Catholics Read the Bible?—The Modern Woman—Visitation of the Sick—How I should Receive My God, etc.

"For preachers in a hurry, unable to consult theological treatises, and forced to get matter at once, these sermons by Father Holland will be found useful. They are clear, precise, suggestive, and the synopsis prefixed to each discourse will present lines of thought which can easily be drawn out in the pulpit. For an overworked priest, a peep into this volume on Saturday night would be a boon and a blessing."—*Catholic Times.*

MOEHLER'S SYMBOLISM.

SYMBOLISM;

OR,

Exposition of the Doctrinal Differences between Catholics and Protestants, as evinced by their Symbolical Writings,

By DR. JOHN ADAM MOEHLER.

Translated from the German by JAMES BURTON ROBERTSON.

FIFTH EDITION. *London,* 1906.

8vo, cloth, NEW - - - - - - **6s. net.**

ST. JOHN DAMASCENE
(A.D. 750).

TREATISE ON HOLY IMAGES

TO WHICH IS ADDED

THREE SERMONS ON THE ASSUMPTION,

Translated from the Original Greek by
MARY H. ALLIES
(Author of "Leaves from S. Chrysostom," etc.),

1898.

Crown 8vo, cloth - - - - - - **2s. net.**

"A work that will be read with much interest, especially at the present time, when Anglicanism is passing through such a critical phase in regard to the position sacred images should occupy in the churches. The treatise to which we refer is entitled 'St. John Damascene on Holy Images,' and is now for the first time published in English (translated from the original Greek by Mary A. Allies)."—*Catholic Record.*

"This book is as a useful weapon in the hands of those who fight for the Catholic doctrines on image honour and devotion to Mary against unbelievers. The former part is largely wrought in with opinions of holy doctors and saints —the latter, dealing with the Assumption, clearly, though learnedly, proves the doctrine of devotion to our Lady to have existed from the remotest ages of the Christian era, and points out the, as it were, necessity of the same. A valuable addition, indeed, to a library of patristic writings.'—*The Universe.*

EDMUND BISHOP

ON THE

HISTORY OF THE CHRISTIAN ALTAR

(Reprinted from the "Downside Review"),

1905.

(31 pp.) 8vo, sewed   -   **8d. net.**

WORKS BY JOHN ORLEBAR PAYNE.

THE ENGLISH CATHOLIC NONJURORS OF 1715.

Being a Summary of the Register of their Estates, with Genealogical and other Notes, and an appendix of Unpublished Documents in the Public Record Office.

BY

JOHN ORLEBAR PAYNE, M.A.

In one vol, demy 8vo, cloth - - - **6s net.**

" Should interest others than the genealogist and historian."
Saturday Review.

" A useful contribution to our Catholic history."—*Tablet.*

" Mr. Payne is to be congratulated on having executed a laborious and useful undertaking in a very creditable manner." — *Morning Post.*

" Every student of the history of our nation, or of families which compose it, cannot but be grateful for a book such as we have here."— *Dublin Review.*

" Another solid contribution to the documentary sources recently put into print relating to the history of Roman Catholics in England. " *Scotsman.*

" An interesting addition to the antiquarian library."—*British Quarterly Review.*

"From first to last full of social interest, and biographical details for which we may search in vain elsewhere." —*Antiquarian Magazine.*

St. Paul's Cathedral in the Time of King Edward VI.

Being a short Account of its Treasures, from a document in the Public Record Office.

EDITED BY

J. ORLEBAR PAYNE.

8vo, cloth - - - - - - - **1s. 6d. net.**

RECORDS OF THE ENGLISH CATHOLICS OF 1715.

Compiled from Original Documents and Edited by
JOHN ORLEBAR PAYNE,

Demy 8vo, cloth - - - - - - **4s. net.**

"A book of the kind Mr. Payne has given us would have astonished Bishop Milner or Dr. Lingard. They would have treasured it, for both of them knew the value of minute fragments of historical information. The Editor has derived nearly the whole of the information which he has given from unprinted sources."—*Tablet.*

"These simple records speak eloquently of the sufferings endured by our forefathers in the Faith, at a time when martyrdom was passed, and will remain as a memorial long prized, not only by the particular families, whose names appear in it, but by the great family of Catholics in England"—*Weekly Register.*

OLD ENGLISH CATHOLIC MISSIONS.

Compiled wholly from Original Documents in Somerset House, with complete Index,
BY JOHN ORLEBAR PAYNE.

(xxv and 122 pp.), demy 8vo, cloth - **3s. net.**

"A book to hunt about in for curious odds and ends."—*Saturday Review.*

"These registers tell us in their too brief records, teeming with interest for all their scantiness, many a tale of patient heroism in the days when the priest would drive to Mass disguised as a carter. . . . We must express our praise of the style in which the book has been brought out, which leaves nothing to be desired."—*Tablet.*

S. ANSELMI *(Archiep. Cantuar., A.D. MCIX.).*

CUR DEUS HOMO?

CUM PREFATIO. LOND., 1896.

12mo, cloth - - - - - - - **1s. net.**

THE LIFE OF
ST. JOHN OF THE CROSS

Of the Order of Our Lady of Mt. Carmel,

BORN 1542, DIED 1591.

Compiled from all his Spanish Biographers and from other sources.

TRANSLATED AND EDITED BY DAVID LEWIS, M.A.

In 1 thick vol, cr. 8vo (over 300 pp.), cloth extra,
2s. net.

" Mr. Lewis's Life of St. John of the Cross is no mere sketch, but a finished picture from the hand of one who knew the Catholic aspects of Spain in the sixteenth century better than any other English writer." *Dublin Review.*

"In this volume we have the gist of the best lives of St. John of the Cross, from that of Fra Joseph of Jesus to that of Garnica, 1893. The deep human interest of the life of the great mystic loses nothing in the hands of Mr. Lewis."—*Cath. University Bulletin.*

" A very admirable work, which we warmly commend to our readers, and which is well calculated to stimulate the study of Hagiography."—*Cath. Times.*

Mr. Lewis' Life of the saint is full, in fact, of matter which will amply repay thoughtful and careful study, and can be warmly recommended to all persons who are not already cognisant of its purport. . . . The book is capitally printed in clear type on good paper."—*Tablet.*

The Life of Dom Bartholomew of the Martyrs,

Religious of the Order of St. Dominic, Archbishop of Braga, in Portugal.

By LADY HERBERT.

Translated from the biographies by FR. LOUIS of Grenada and others.

In 1 thick vol, demy 8vo - **4s. 6d. net.**

"Lady Herbert's large Life of this wonderful servant of God—Dom Bartholomew of the Martyrs—has become a standard work on the ecclesiastical spirit, and a *perfect treasury* for Priests and Bishops."—*Bishop of Salford.*

Agostino da Montefeltro

(O.S.F.)

Conferences at Rome, Florence and Milan.

1888-91.

TRANSLATED BY

C. AUBREY ANSELL AND H. DALBY GALLI.

Two volumes, crown 8vo, cloth extra, **5s.** net.

Only complete English edition.

———

CONTENTS :

Volume I.—Existence of God—Who God is—True Conception of Man—The Soul in Science and Art—The Immortality of the Soul—The End of Life and Religion—St Joseph—Sorrow—The True Religion—Sources of Unbelief—The Working Classes—Mary.

Volume II.—Jesus Christ—Christ the God Man—Doctrine of Jesus Christ Purgatory—Love of Jesus—Our Faith—Hope—The Supernatural—Sunday Rest—Faith and Science—The Eucharist—Confession and Penance Prejudice againt Religion--The Passion, etc.

———

The only faithful and unemasculated edition in English. It is neither " Adapted," " Abridged," or " Selected."

With the special approbation of the late Cardinal Archbishop of Westminster.

———

" The subjects chosen by the Preacher are of the simplest consisting chiefly of bold and forcible defence of the Christian Faith against Materialism, eloquent and fervid appeals to the people for truthfulness and honesty in social intercourse and earnest exhortations to purity of family life."

" The simplicity of his premises, the clear logic of his arguments and the soundness of his conclusions, united with a certain magnetism of manner and intense sympathy with the *people*, are the evident causes of his great success, and have placed him high amongst the great preachers of the Century. He has been already alluded to as ' The Italian Lacordaire.' "

THE HISTORY AND ANTIQUITIES OF THE ANGLO-SAXON CHURCH,

Containing an Account of its Origin, Doctrines, Worship, Revenues, and Clerical and Monastic Institutions,

By Dr. JOHN LINGARD.

A New Edition, in 2 vols, crown 8vo, cloth extra, 6s. net.

HEADS OF CONTENTS :

The Conversion of the Britons and Saxons—Succession and Duties of Bishops—Church Government—Anglo-Saxon Clergy—Anglo-Saxon Monks—Donations to the Church—Religious Worship—Religious Practices—Literature—Decline of Piety and Learning—Reform by St. Dunstan—Foreign Missions—Notes, &c., &c.

" This valuable work opened the eyes of the public to the misrepresentations of the ancient English Church by certain Protestant writers, and inaugurated more truthful historical research."—*Gillow.*

"Whoever reads ' Soames' or ' Sharon Turner' should also read Lingard."

DOM PROSPER GUERANGER.

THE LITURGICAL YEAR

Translated from the French by the Benedictines of Stanbrook Abbey, 1900-3.

Complete Set, 15 vols, cr. 8vo, cloth   -   -   £3 10s. net.

S. TERESA'S LIFE
Written by Herself,

And Translated from the Spanish by DAVID LEWIS.

Third Edition enlarged.

Re-edited, with numerous additional Notes, and a new
Introduction by the

Rev. Father BENEDICT ZIMMERMAN,
Prior O.C.D., of Wincanton Priory, Somerset.

1904.

Thick 8vo, cloth, extra, gilt top, new   -   **8s. net.**

This édition is handsomely printed in new pica type, and contains over
twenty-seven pages of new matter and a new photogravure portrait of the
Saint after the celebrated picture in the Convent of the Carmelites at Seville.

Father Zimmerman's valuable Revisions and Additions to Mr. Lewis's
fine translation render it by far the Best and Most Complete Edition of this
celebrated book that has yet appeared.

BERNARD W. KELLY.

XXV. Short Sermons on Doctrinal and Historical Subjects,
With a Synopsis of each Sermon. 1907.

Thick cr. 8vo, cloth   -   -   ·   -   -   -   **4s.**

Contents :—The Immortality of the Soul —Faith and its Exemplification
in the Magi—Prayer—The Genius of Christianity—Dogmatic Teaching of
the New Testament—Doctrinal Aspect of the Early Church—The Communion
of Saints—Christian Symbolism—The Holy Mother of God—The Sacred
Heart—The Scourging of Our Lord—The Cross—Confirmation—The Sacrament of Penance—The Blessed Eucharist —Holy Matrimony—The Supremacy
of the Holy See—St. Patrick—The Monks of the West—The Spiritual
Aspects of Reading—The Catholic Revival in England—Conformity to the
Will of God—Our Last End—Purgatory —The Last Judgment.

ST. TERESA.

THE INTERIOR CASTLE,

OR, THE MANSIONS.

Translated from the Autograph of St. Teresa, by the Benedictines of Stanbrook Abbey, revised with Notes by BENEDICT ZIMMERMAN. 1906.

Crown 8vo, cloth - - - - - **4s.**

The Letters of Saint Teresa

TRANSLATED FROM THE ORIGINAL SPANISH BY JOHN DALTON.

Crown 8vo, cloth extra - - - - **2s. net.**

DR. DANIEL ROCK.

THE HIERURGIA,

OR THE HOLY SACRIFICE OF THE MASS,

With Notes and Dissertations elucidating its Doctrines and Ceremonies.

A New and thoroughly revised Edition, with many new Illustrations.

Edited, with a Preface, by W. H. JAMES WEALE.

Two vols, 8vo, cloth - - - - **10s. 6d. net.**

"The name of Mr. Weale on the title page is a guarantee that the work of editing has been carefully and conscientiously performed. An examination of the volumes now issued and a comparison of the first edition has convinced us, that so far from this being a mere reprint, there is hardly a page which does not manifest the work of the Editor."—*Tablet.*

HOW TO PRAY.

By PÈRE GROU

Third Edition.

TRANSLATED FROM THE FRENCH BY TERESA FITZGERALD.

EDITED BY RICHARD F. CLARKE, S.J.

Thick crown 8vo, cloth   -   -   -   -   **3s. net.**

CONTENTS : God alone can Teach us How to Pray - On the Multiplicity of Vocal Prayers—On the Efficacy of Prayer—On Continual Prayer—On Prayer in Common—The Lord's Prayer.

" We welcome Teresa Fitzgerald's translation, ' *How to Pray.*' Now that it can be obtained in an English dress it should be studied by all. The translation is both smooth and accurate." – *The Guardian.*

" This book is likely to be of special use to persons who have allowed rules of prayer to cramp their devotions. and with whom regularity has become a wrong kind of formality."—*Ch. Quarterly*

" We like this little book a thousand times better than most translations ; and we share the conviction that it will be a source of comfort and encourage- ment to every reader." –*Ave Maria.*

" A beautiful book and a useful book. It is intended for earnest souls and for prayerful souls. A very valuable treatise, nearly every part of which is as true and as good for the uses of the Christian life in one Church as in another."—*Churchman.*

" Father Grou in this work gives wise suggestions as to the proper mode of praying. . . . his directions will prove highly profitable to all who adopt them. The work has been well translated."—*Catholic Times.*

" Many devoutly inclined persons who read these pages will learn much from them . . . to comfort and encourage in their struggles against aridity in prayer."—*American Eccl. Review.*

MEDITATIONS UPON THE LOVE OF GOD.

TRANSLATED FROM THE FRENCH OF PÈRE GROU.

(174 *pp.*) 18mo, cloth extra   -   -   -   **Is. 6d. net.**

S. THOMÆ AQUINAS.

Summa Theologica ad emendatiores editiones impressa et accuratissime recognita.

Romæ Typographia Senatus, 1894.

6 thick vols, 8vo, half morocco   -   -   -   **£1 16s.**

URBS ET ORBIS,

OR

THE POPE AS BISHOP AND AS PONTIFF

By WM. HUMPHREY, S.J.

Thick crown 8vo, cloth - - - **6s. 6d. net.**

CONTENTS :

(1) Elements in the Church of Divine Institution—(2) Elements in the Church of Human Institution—(3) The Senate of the Pope—(4) The Household of the Pope—(5) The Diocese of Rome—(6) Secret Roman Congregations—(7) Papal Blessing.

" The purpose of the present volume is to set forth the Papacy in action, with some account of the machinery by means of which the supreme Pontiff has governed and governs the visible Church."—*Preface.*

Elements of Religious Life,

By WM. HUMPHREY, S.J.

Second Edition, revised and enlarged.

Thick 8vo, cloth - - - - - **9s. net.**

This edition contains translations of the Apostolic Constitution *Conditæ* of December 8, 1900, in which Leo XIII. gives rules both for Diocesan Institutes, and for Institutes approved by the Holy See ; and of the Decree *Perpensis Temporum*, whereby Leo XIII. on May 3rd, 1902, extended to religious women the Decrees of Pius IX. with regard to religious men.

This edition has also an additional chapter on Congregations of Sisters under simple vows. This treats of their foundation, approbation, admission and dismissal of subjects, vows, government, manner of life, superiors, officials, etc., and brings the legislation on the subject down to date.

CONSCIENCE AND LAW

OR PRINCIPLES OF HUMAN CONDUCT,

By WM. HUMPHREY, S.J.

Second Edition.

Crown 8vo, cloth - - - - - - - **3s. net.**

CONTENTS :

Human Responsibility—Conscience—Law—Dispensations and Privileges—Justice and Right—Restitution.

"A book from Father Humphrey's pen is sure to be not only well written but of practical utility Let the forward reformers and the lawgivers study these chapters on *Human Responsibility. Conscience, Law, Dispensations and Privileges, Justice, Right and Restitution ;* 'they will find no vague verbiage, no merely plausible argumentation, but only simple, direct logic, with every term well defined in advance, and every conclusion reached through legitimate forcing of common reason. To the theologian, especially the priest who is to act as judge, whether in the confessional or in public administration, we could recommend no better work."—*American Ecclesiastical Review.*

"This is a book to be studied, not simply read. Within the small compass of 226 pages the learned author has compressed the pith and marrow of a whole volume of Moral Theology. . . . It will not only be found serviceable as a class-book in Colleges, but may be read with great profit by all educated readers."—*Catholic Times*

HIS DIVINE MAJESTY,

OR THE LIVING GOD,

By WM. HUMPHREY, S.J.

Thick crown 8vo, cloth - - - **6s. 6d. net.**

HEADS OF CHAPTERS :

Man's Knowledge of God's Existence, Man's Knowledge of what God is, The Essence and the Attributes of God, The Absolute Properties of the Divine Essence, The Negative Properties of the Divine Essence, God's Knowledge, God's Sincere Will of Man's Salvation, God the One Creator, God as the Author of Nature, God as the Author of the Supernatural, The Paradise of God's Creation, The Inner Life of God.

THE ETERNAL SACRIFICE

TRANSLATED FROM THE FRENCH OF

CHARLES DE CONDREN.

(207 pp.), cr. 8vo, cloth   -   -   -   -   **2s. 6d. net.**

PART I.—The Priesthood of Jesus Christ.

Of Sacrifice in General—Sacrifice of the Christian Religion—The Design of God in the reconciliation of men and of the qualities of the priest who should be the mediator.— That Jesus Christ is a priest according to the order of Melchisedeck, not according to the order of Aaron—When and how Jesus Christ fulfilled the functions of a priest—Of the difference which exists between the sacrifice of the Cross, that of the Mass, and that of Heaven.

PART II.—Symbolism of Christian Worship.

The Holy of Holies a figure of the Bosom of God ; the entrance of the high priest, a figure of the entry of Jesus Christ into that adorable temple— Jesus Christ is the Altar; visible altars only figurative—Proofs drawn from the Canon of the Mass and from the Gospel that Jesus Christ is the true altar— That the Holy Ghost is the fire of the sacrifice of Jesus Christ.

Charles de Condren, General of the *O*ratory, was one of the most distinguished Ecclesiastics of France in the reign of Henri IV. His most important book, which was published after his death, is entitled " L'Idèe du Sacerdoce de Jésus Christ," of which the present volume ("The Eternal Sacrifice") is a translation.

He was the Spiritual Father and Guide of the Saintly M. Olier (Founder of the College of S. Sulpice), who said of him that perhaps no man ever penetrated more profoundly into the sublimest mysteries of the faith, while St. Jane Francis de Chantal, comparing him with St. Francis de Sales, says, " It seemed to me that God had given our blessed Father to teach Men, but that he had made Père de Condren fit to teach Angels."

NOW READY.   Price **7s. 6d. net.**

In one handsome volume, 8vo, cloth.

The Ascent of Mount Carmel

BY

ST. JOHN OF THE CROSS.

Translated by DAVID LEWIS, with Corrections and a Prefatory Essay on Carmelite Mysticism by the V. R. PRIOR ZIMMERMANN, O.C.D.

ST. THOMAS AQUINAS IN ENGLISH.

———

A Compendium of the Pars Prima of the Summa Theologica of St. Thomas Aquinas.

By BERARDUS BONJOANNES, A.D. 1560.

TRANSLATED INTO ENGLISH.

With an Introduction and an Appendix Explanatory of SCHOLASTIC TERMS

By R. R. CARLO FALCINI,
Vicar-General of the Diocese of Fiesole, Italy.

Revised by *The Rev. Father* WILFRID LESCHER, O P.

In one handsome volume.   8vo, cloth extra.   Price **6s. 6d. net.**
1906.

"Though this portion of the great edifice of Theology may justly be considered as *fundamental* in its relation to the *Prima Secundæ;* the *Secunda Secundæ* and the *7ertia Pars;* still it would be a mistake to imagine that there is anything about it unfinished or wanting in logical accuracy or precision of sequence," etc.—*Vaughan's Life of St. Thomas of Aquin.*

34295

Lightning Source UK Ltd.
Milton Keynes UK
UKOW06f2213150915

258703UK00008B/188/P